Erling Jorstad

The Politics of Moralism

The New Christian Right in American Life

AUGSBURG Publishing House • Minneapolis

To Emily and Jim White

269.0973
J769
82070128

THE POLITICS OF MORALISM: THE NEW
CHRISTIAN RIGHT IN AMERICAN LIFE

Copyright © 1981 Augsburg Publishing House

Library of Congress Catalog Card No. 81-65641

International Standard Book No. 0-8066-1877-9

Scripture quotations unless otherwise noted are from the
Revised Standard Version of the Bible, copyright 1946, 1952,
and 1971 by the Division of Christian Education of the
National Council of Churches.

Many people have helped in the preparation of this book; I
can list only a few here. Grateful acknowledgement is made
to the American Jewish Committee, Institute of Human Relations, for permission to let me quote from its study "The New
Right." The materials quoted are in Chapters 9 and 11.
Thanks in abundance to Lois Geistfeld, a one-person clipping
service, commentator, and typist extraordinaire. The book is
dedicated to Emily and Jim White; would that everyone had
such good friends.

Manufactured in the United States of America

Contents

One

The Emergence of the
New Christian Right

Will Rogers once remarked that the surest way to get into an argument with a fellow countryman was to tell him your recipe for how religion and politics should mix. His homely truism embodies a profound truth about Americans. While they may not be consistently well-informed about the issues of the day, they will vigorously deny that anyone else knows more than they do about the proper blend of religion and politics in America.

THE 1980 CAMPAIGN

In the late 1970s this argument, as old as America itself, broke out across the country with new urgency, rancor, and divisiveness. The immediate cause was the national campaign of 1980. But campaigns have always been characterized by sharp debate, acrimonious rhetoric, and partisan squabbling, after which the contestants join together to continue the work of the republic.

By Election Day, 1980, however some new, often explosive ingredients had been added into the familiar recipe of religion and politics. A substantial number of smoothly organized, energetic, and well-financed evangelicals and fundamentalists, clergy and laity alike, stormed directly and boldly into the many elective campaigns. Their speeches talked of "America's last chance," "the judgments of God," of crisis, of the 1980s as "The Decade of Destiny." Decisions, they exhorted, would have to be made right now by public officials if this republic were to be saved from destruction.

Such expressions are hardly new in history, but the 1980 campaign produced original and far-reaching changes in American religious and political life. *Right now,* the indictment read, America must turn back its foolish ways, repent of its immoral deeds, turn out of office those who would not stand for morality, and seek once again the restoration of those principles on which the nation was founded. America was on the verge of moral collapse, but God had given it one last chance. At least there were those citizens, in this book called the "New Christian Right," who knew *what* had gone wrong and knew *how* to prevent disaster.

The question arose: what was wrong? The New Christian Right drew up an extensive list. At the top were several interrelated crises: the results of the 1973 Supreme Court decision on abortion, demands by homosexuals for civil rights, the Supreme Court's prohibition of religious exercises in public schools, the Equal Rights Amendment, the accessibility of pornography, and, in a different realm, the alleged decline of American prestige and power abroad due to a weakening military posture compared to increasing Soviet might. Here were issues public officials could correct; here were moral dilemmas which could be resolved. Salvation was to be found not only at the altar, but at the ballot box. With the right men, highly moral men, in high public office, America could yet be redeemed to continue its God-given destiny.

5

As the call for repentance and revival mounted throughout 1980, one astounding feature came to dominate the movement. The leaders and supporters were largely from the evangelical and fundamentalist wings of American Protestantism, with some conservative Jews, Protestants, and Catholics alongside. So unexpected to the professional political observers was the entrance of this bloc that they did not know quite what to make of it. For decades, even centuries, this segment of the community of faith had earnestly, persistently called on Americans to repent and restore morality in both their public and private lives. But this call had been made almost exclusively through the organized denominations or the local parishes, on a one-to-one basis. Organized political campaigning had been left to the "social gospelers," the "liberals," while they had concentrated on personal evangelism. Their attitude had been: save the seeker's soul, and the morality will follow thereafter.

All this was changed between 1976 and 1980, at least in its public expression. The Carter-Reagan campaign took on a new character because the many evangelicals and fundamentalists, conservative in both their theology and their political priorities, did what politically minded people outside their tradition had done for decades: register, get others to register, ring doorbells for candidates and funds, work through the communications media, stage national rallies, get out the vote. This activity was new, and it was conservative; hence the term in the title "The New Christian Right."[1] The nation had never seen anything quite like it.

On close examination, the New Christian Right stood remarkably united in its commitments and values, its priorities and its long-range objectives. It had a clear, but not tightly disciplined, set of leaders directing its activities. Its formal link to organized politics, the National Conservative Political Action Committee (NCPAC) maintained close ties to the Republican Party.

THE PREACHERS AND THE MAILERS

On closer examination, however, the means and structures for implementing the programs showed wide diversity. Two kinds of religio-political organizations became highly evident, both remarkably well-organized, strongly financed, and clear in their objectives. The first was the "electronic church," especially those celebrity ministers whose names in the last four years had become household words: Pat Robertson, Jim Bakker, Jerry Falwell, and James Robison. The second group lacked their visibility but commanded a commensurate amount of influence. These were the computerized direct-mail agencies such as Moral Majority, Christian Voice, Religious Roundtable, and the National Christian Action Coalition, along with several smaller groups.

The television preachers, with their several formats, presented the compelling issues of the day to growing millions of viewers. They understood their ministry to be evangelism, bringing the message to people who had been waiting to hear it and were willing to support it to the amount of about one million dollars a week per program. The direct-mail solicitors, with their several formats, reached some 20,000,000 voters with their agenda of moral issues for the campaign. They also prepared "moral report cards" which rated the votes of national lawmakers against their own standards of what constituted a "moral" or "immoral" vote on a key public issue. These report cards were widely circulated in the states of targeted senators and representatives whom the New Christian Right wanted to see defeated.

Neither the political oratory nor the targets or report

cards were original contributions to American political campaigning. What was almost totally new was the fact that the work was being done by a sizeable portion of the populace which had studiously shunned such activity before. But now, in 1980, their leaders had convinced them of the gravity of the crisis facing America; this was no time to stand on tradition. God-fearing Americans must organize, campaign, and vote as a united bloc.

MORALITY VERSUS MORALISM

The theme brought home in every speech, every sermon, every pamphlet, every request for funds was that of saving America by a return to what the leaders called its traditional morality. As this book will attempt to show, the New Christian Right created in those years (and for the foreseeable future) "the politics of moralism." Moralism is distinct from morality, at least as it came into usage in the late 1970s. *Morality* can be defined as the rightness or wrongness of human actions.[2] The centuries-old question, of course, is who decides what is wrong or right: professional priests, holy men, sacred writings, or trial-and-error experience? All of these and other sources are at our disposal today for defining morality. But authentic morality hesitates to place too much authority in any one person or group of persons because, as Reinhold Niebuhr reminded us, "Man is a finite and contingent creature, with some sense of universal value transcending his own existence but unfortunately inclined to endow the contingent values of his life or culture, of his truth or loyalty, with an absolute significance which it does not deserve." Morality allows us to choose between right and wrong, but our finite creatureliness gives us at best the chance to do so "through a glass darkly."

Moralism as it stands in the early 1980s means something else. It is not the direct opposite of morality, but something of a deviation. Moralism also treats what is right and what is wrong. It differs from morality in these respects: (1) it posits only one right moral action to any ethical question because (2) its authority is based on that view of Scripture which claims it is inerrant, infallible, and verbally inspired entirely without "error" in its original. Those Scriptures yield only one answer to each question. Those persons who accept that view of authority are the people qualified to decide what action is right and what is wrong, what is moral and what is immoral. (3) They can measure in quantifiable terms (such as voting report cards) the degree of morality of a person, in this case a public lawmaker by choosing a select number of public issues and controversies on which the lawmaker must vote. Since those who speak with absolute authority have the moral answers they turn morality into moralism because they state they have the answers; those who disagree with them may not necessarily be "immoral" but they are not "moral."

Moralism further embodies a particular world view. It understands that the moral answers to the questions perplexing mankind since earliest times are known, that no new or revised moralistic teachings will be forthcoming from the Author of morality because all revelation from him is full, complete, and binding.

Moralism, then, is not morality because it assumes the validity of one judgmental answer to every moral question, and it assumes that humans are wise enough to understand what God intends for each of them in every instance of life. How could it be otherwise? Could God teach that there are several reasonably moral answers to each question, with each of us free to pick and choose as we please? Of course not, say the moralists. God does

9

not mock, and thus he has given us absolute answers. We know them, says the New Christian Right. We can state them in language everyone understands, and we can use them to measure the moral behavior of everyone around us.

The New Christian Right, then, came to employ the "politics of moralism" against those lawmakers with whom they disagreed. Their moral report cards were the instruments to conduct a political campaign, to measure a person's morality. Moral issues and answers, over which public leaders had disagreed, were made political tools for votes and funds. The New Christian Right, as we will see, conceded freely that not every major issue was instantly divisible into right and wrong. But on those issues which the leaders selected for evaluation, no compromise was possible.

Having realized they could not save America by working only through political evangelism and church activities, the New Christian Right chose to go public. And they helped transform American life, a story by early 1981 clearly visible, but still not yet complete. Hence this book is a first account of their achievements: the history, activities, beliefs, and results of the preachers and the mailers. Since this book is written so soon after the 1980 election, some of its emphases and accents will become dated within a few years. Given that risk, the story of the impact of the New Christian Right on American life is worth telling.

UNSOLVED QUESTIONS

The emergence of this movement raises questions which cannot be resolved here: In a religiously pluralistic society, such as the United States, how can the standards of morality necessary for any civilized society best be determined and, if necessary, amended? Should major moral issues be settled at the ballot boxes? Are constitutional amendments a better route to travel? Is the nation, the body politic, the appropriate agency for preserving Judeo-Christian morality? In a nation upholding its own understanding of the separation of church and state, what can denominations do to maintain the foundations of high moral conduct? Can the Christian faith establish a national consensus for accepting one code of morality for all its citizens? Do we want such a code? What reply can be made to those, in this case the New Christian Right, who claim their religious liberty is being violated by current practices on abortion, bans on prayer and Bible reading in public schools, the Equal Rights Amendment, and other issues? Are not those who take positions other than the New Christian Right also practicing a "politics of moralism"? Today certain practices such as abortion or civil rights for homosexuals extend a certain kind of freedom for those involved in them. At what point do these practices, which may or may not directly or even indirectly involve an individual, become issues on which she or he has the right to dictate how others should behave?

These questions will be the foundation of the discussion in this book. Some tentative answers will be suggested in the last chapter. Before that can be done, however, we will look in some detail, on the rise, practice, message, and effectiveness of the New Christian Right in American life.

Two

The Christian Right:
Transformation
from Old to New

"Congress shall make no law respecting an establishment of religion; or prohibit the free exercise thereof." This, the first of the several great rights in the Bill of Rights, is today being put to an intense trial. Throughout American history it has never been free from controversy, but today's strain embraces several unique ingredients for which earlier precedents yield little guidance. The freedom of religion clause has become something which the Founding Fathers never envisioned for it. Their clear intention was to prevent the creation of any official governmental or state church in the United States as had existed in Britain. Further, they explicitly prohibited any public or private agency from preventing the citizens from expressing their religious understanding as they saw fit. Or citizens could be free to make no religious expression at all.

Over the decades, with some notable exceptions, the freedom of religion clause served the purposes for which it was written. By compromise and goodwill, mutual trust and flexibility, Americans avoided a state church. And despite injustice and suffering inflicted on some religious minorities, an enormous number and variety of religious organizations found the freedom to express their beliefs; those who chose to express none were also protected in their choice. In contrast to other nations in Christendom, the United States had no "holy war," no extended physical conflict among religious bodies. The freedom of religion clause kept alive the aims of those who placed it into the Constitution.[1]

Today's trial emerges directly out of several of the profound social, political, and technological changes of the recent past, changes the Founding Fathers could not have anticipated. The political arena has become the battleground from which the populace expects solutions to the most agonizing, uncompromisable moral questions. Political answers in the American system need cooperation and compromise to succeed, but they are not available today. Rather, as in the 1850s over the uncompromisable moral issue of slavery, public opinion is growing more divisive, more bitter, less open to compromise. This time the issues are abortion, gay rights, the feminist movement, and increased armaments—to name the top of the list.[2] Today, as never before in American history, voter opinion is being organized, and channeled to the lawmakers with great success by new, sophisticated technology: computers can produce an instant avalanche of mail to Congress or the state legislatures on a specific issue, most of those today being the no-compromise moral dilemmas. In years past many divisive moral questions were mediated by the organized churches; today they too are in turmoil and controversy rather than being agencies of reconciliation.

THE BEGINNING OF REALIGNMENT

These changes, which obviously did not appear on the scene overnight, could well lead to a new alignment of organized church bodies. The first visible evidence that significant realignment was possible appeared first in the early 1960s. Then too, as in our day, volatile moral issues riveted public attention on the conflicts bursting out. The most far-reaching controversies centered on civil rights for minorities, equal rights for women, the antiwar movement, student militancy on the campuses, and continuing strains in foreign policy with the Soviet Union.

None of these battles yielded to rapid or simple answers for the politically liberal government in Washington. Out of conviction and impatience, a vigorous politically conservative counterattack started attracting more of the voters' attention. It was headed both by intellectuals, such as William F. Buckley Jr., and political leaders, such as Senator Barry Goldwater. By 1964 they became strong enough to capture the Republican presidential nomination for the Arizona senator. Conservative leaders were convinced a "silent majority" of conservative voters was out there, waiting for a genuine article, such as Goldwater, to take command. On such they staked their hopes and with such they failed. No such majority existed and the incumbent president, Lyndon Johnson, won a staggering victory.

THE POLITICS OF DOOMSDAY

Yet not all conservatives stood with Buckley's programs or those of Senator Goldwater. A small, then growing, number of highly energetic fundamentalists made their contribution to the debates of the 1960s in a movement best described as "the politics of doomsday." [3] Theologically fundamentalist, politically on the far right, ecclesiastically devoted to total separation from the smallest hint of "apostasy"—thousands of believers followed the leadership of Carl McIntire or Billy James Hargis (or some lesser imitator) to demand the restoration of their morality into public life.

Much of the appeal of these spokesmen came from their outspoken, often harsh, verbal and printed criticism of national leaders, such as President John F. Kennedy, Dr. Martin Luther King Jr., and ecumenical leaders such as Eugene Carson Blake and James Pike. The "fundamentalists of the far right" also found strong objections to the theology and programs of the evangelicals, such as Billy Graham or the journal *Christianity Today*. From these and a host of other sources they detected an internal conspiracy by Americans themselves to deliver this nation first into liberalism, then to socialism, and finally and inevitably into Communism. Once the slide had started, it was irreversible.

Evidence for the internal conspiracy was found by the leaders to be everywhere: in the Oval Office, in mainline denominations, in the curricula of elementary schools, in almost all seminaries except their own (Bob Jones, Faith, and a handful of others). Communist influence had permeated the Supreme Court, the lesson plans of the Methodist Church Sunday schools, professional sports—the list could be extended at length.

The leaders demanded that unless America returned to the standards of righteousness which they outlined, this nation would be destroyed from within, and then only the End Times could preserve the few Christians who remained.[4] Their program constituted a "Christian Right," distinct from the moderate conservatives.

As the '60s wound down, amidst all of its turmoil and confusion, the Christian Right became increasingly isolated from the mainstream of conservative dissent. The

15

McIntires, Hargises, and others spent considerable time arguing among themselves; their guilt-by-association assaults on nationally prominent leaders (such as Graham) lost them credibility in public opinion. And, compared to what would be the New Christian Right, they did not have at their disposal the two great technological instruments the new rightists would use to achieve success: television and direct mailings by computers. The older far right did utilize extensive radio broadcasting, personal appearances, and hand-processed mailings. Yet those items failed to carry their messages into the markets where, later, the New Right would attract far larger support. By the early 1970s the politics of doomsday was largely a memory.

Yet, despite its demise, it planted seed for later harvesting. Younger industrious evangelical and fundamentalist leaders had observed how rapidly these earlier spokesmen had moved into national prominence, the power they commanded, the audiences they could organize, solicit, and direct. The phenomenon of such ultrafundamentalist preachers becoming national celebrities was indeed something new in American life; those who would create the politics of moralism waited for their moment.

Of special interest for the New Christian Right was the employment by George Wallace of Richard Vigurie, a professional fund raiser in Washington, D.C. Once on the staff of Texas Senator John Tower, Vigurie had achieved his first prominence as executive director of Young Americans for Freedom. By 1965 he had started his first direct mail activities. For Wallace, Vigurie was able to collect thousands of names of donors and their special interest in issues. A few years later he would build on that collection.[5]

THE SEVENTIES

Decades, such as the 1960s or 1970s take on distinctive, if over-simplified, characteristics. The "liberal" or "reformist" tendencies of the '60s evaporated quickly during the '70s. The high hopes for peace and freedom, the dreams of minorities, the resistance from the Oval Office towards continuing the liberal Great Society programs all helped to color the '70s a different hue.

During those years the Supreme Court handed down several major decisions which helped increase evangelical/fundamentalist frustration over the direction of American life. In 1973 the Court greatly expanded the kinds of legal abortions allowed; it upheld busing of school children to achieve racial balance; it continued to prohibit religious exercises, such as Bible reading and prayer, in public school. It gave extensive flexibility to publishers and movie producers, who responded with what many thought were pornographic materials. Efforts by Congressmen to override these decisions by constitutional amendments were either bottled up in committees or defeated on the floor.

Beyond that, stories of chislers of public welfare funds spread across the newspapers; the mass media discovered "a sexual revolution" was rampant and had solid figures on illegitimate births, increases in cohabiting, and venereal disease to prove it. Increasing numbers of Americans were asking, what is going on?

One answer was offered by the most prominent evangelical in the land. Reading the signs, Billy Graham decided that to help turn back the galloping decline of America, the citizenry should be made to feel proud of their country. Patriotism should be tapped as a means of regaining what he and his supporters believed was the original purpose of the Founding Fathers. With much

17

preparation, Graham led on July 4, 1970, in Washington an "Honor America" rally. It attempted to reinstate a sense of pride in America's achievements, a sense of virtue and self-control over moral temptations, and a rededicated faith in God. Graham called on Americans to "sing again! America needs to celebrate again! America needs to wave the flag again! Proudly gather around the flag and all that it stands for." [6]

As the decade unfolded, mass rallies for God, country, and morality increased in number. Bill Bright, founder and directior of Campus Crusade, headed up the first "Explo 72" gathering in Dallas. Over 80,000 young Christians participated in a week-long crusade of services, workshops, and sharing. Whatever long-range impact such meetings might have had, they did indicate that some new spirit, something energetic and aggressive, was alive and spreading in the evangelical world.

Soon additional convincing evidence appeared indicating that the older mainline denominations were slowly losing both members and resources. At the same time the evangelical, fundamentalist, and several sectarian bodies were growing at an astounding rate. Their most careful observer, Dean Kelley, concluded their growth was the direct result of their demands for moral rectitude, commitment, self-sacrifice, and assent to traditional, uncomplicated doctrine.[7]

More signs poured in of an evangelical resurgence. Attendance at Christian day schools, at Bible schools, at evangelical colleges and seminaries rose dramatically, while declining in nonaffiliated institutions. Sales of evangelical books grew at an amazing pace, jumping 26 percent in 1976 over 1975. Sales of records by Christian rock musicians increased substantially. Membership in church bodies such as the Seventh Day Adventists, Jehovah's Witnesses, and the Mormons grew increasingly each year. Self-help seminars led by evangelicals, such as Basic Youth Conflicts (Bill Gothard) and Total Woman (Marabelle Morgan), attracted hundreds of thousands of participants annually.[8]

Clearly at work was a growing public acceptance of the sincerity and dedication of born-again evangelicals. Instead of being relegated to ridicule or isolation, evangelicals now were being widely accepted. Nowhere was this more evident than in the witness of candidate Jimmy Carter of Georgia for the presidency.

Among the several qualities the former governor brought to his candidacy, none was more newsworthy than his open testimony to his religious faith. Although it is impossible to measure accurately how attractive this faith made him to voters, what it accomplished was to make evangelical public witnessing far more respectable than before.[9] This gave evangelicals greater courage and initiative to speak publicly on major issues, a level of participation they had for the most part long avoided.[10]

THE PROFESSIONALS MOVE IN

In other words, evangelicals across the denominational spectrum were finding the presence of larger numbers of like-minded believers. Something of a national constituency or cohesive bloc of voters was taking shape, however dimly. The professional fund raisers and bloc-vote organizers in Washington also noted the same phenomenon; an audience was being created.

As early as 1974 three leaders decided this audience was worth cultivating; each later would become a major voice in the New Christian Right. Best known was Richard Vigurie, who with his fund raising skills offered his programs in nearby Virginia to the emerging National Conservative Political Action Committee (NCPAC); the latter surfaced formally a year later. Secondly was Paul Weyrich, heading the Committee for the Survival of a Free Congress, an early issue-oriented lobby on Capitol Hill. The two were joined by Howard Phillips, a conservative Republican embittered by Watergate and looking for new ways to reenter politics. Much of the funding for the early talks among the three came from Adolph Coors, well-known financier for right-wing causes and a student of Weyrich.

The three at first planned a third party to be headed by a Reagan-Wallace ticket. Each of them offered his specialty: Phillips organized the Conservative Caucus for grassroots politicking, Vigurie headed up the finances, Weyrich worked on the issues. But neither candidate showed interest, and the plan was abandoned. They came back in 1976 with new ideas. From the right wing "think tank," The Heritage Foundation, Weyrich brought together two studies, both of which would serve as models for the 1980 campaign. The first, *The Spirit of '76* was "a handbook for winning elections" with detailed directions for evangelicals showing them how to elect lawmakers who agreed with their moral priorities. The second title was *The Third Century Index,* an evaluation of the voting records of all Senators and Representatives during the 1975 session of Congress based on these criteria: "individual freedom, fiscal responsibility, free competitive enterprise, and Constitutional government based on God's laws—with justice and equity for all." [11] Specific votes by which Congressmen were rated included, among others: mandated school busing, the Panama Canal Treaty, the food-stamp program, federal funding for abortions, and a consumer-advocacy program. *The Third Century Index* showed displeasure with these proposals.[12]

The extent to which national lawmakers voted for or

against these items was used to determine whether they were applying what the direct mailers called "Christian principles" in their voting. Staunchly evangelical Senator Mark Hatfield, for one, received only a 30; and equally staunchly evangelical John Anderson, a 20. On the 0 to 100 scale in the Senate the leading "Christians" were Jesse Helms, 90, Harry Byrd 90, and Strom Thurmond, 80.

Vigurie also pressed ahead with plans to solidify the conservative vote. He told *Sojourners* magazine he was pursuing the "Christian moral voter. The next real major area of growth for the conservative ideology and philosophy is among evangelical people. I would be surprised if in the next year you did not see a massive effort to involve them, utilizing mail and other techniques." [13]

Apart from Vigurie and NCPAC three very small, incipient New Christian Right groups prepared slates of "Christ-centered" candidates for Congress. These included the Christian Freedom Foundation, the Christian Embassy, and Intercessors for America. None had adequate resources or much political savvy. Yet they had broken with past traditions; the next step would be easier to take.[14]

Although tiny by any standard, the Vigurie-Weyrich-Phillips network of nationalistic, conservative fund raisers and voter motivaters showed in the election months of 1976 the pattern they would use with such great success four years later. Concerned voters would write them, or respond to general letters the mailers would send out about gun control, or abortion, or pornography, or religious exercises in public schools, or Soviet militarism. The mailers would send each correspondent a letter, typed by computer, but reading as though it had been dictated directly to that person (even though all the people on, say, gun control received the same letter). The concerned citizen would be asked to make a donation, or attend a rally, or in some other tangible way express interest in this specific issue. Out of this came what Kevin Phillips so aptly labelled "The Balkanization of America," the era of one-issue politics. Some of the soon-to-be founders of the New Christian Right had found ways to raise funds and get votes.[15]

In 1976 evangelical hopes for Carter, the born-again president, were high among fellow believers. None of the direct mail groups had any campaign going against him. These were truly "the years of the Evangelicals" as *Newsweek* labelled them. If an observer doubted that evaluation, he could have looked to another movement spreading across the nation showing how powerful the evangelicals truly were. Known by several names, this movement was most readily recognized as "the electronic church." Its contributions to the politics of moralism and the New Christian Right are so extensive and formidable that we need to examine them in some detail.

_____Three_____

Evangelism
by Electronics:
The Rise of the
Television Churches

During his ministry, Jesus taught and preached to an estimated twenty to thirty thousand people. By the early 1980s, a speaker using electronic communication could address some one billion people at the same time. Using satellite communications, that speaker could be seen live simultaneously by one out of every five persons around the globe.[1]

Evangelism-minded Christians discovered in this transformation an unparalleled opportunity to carry out the great commission of Matthew 28: "Go therefore and make disciples of all nations." Even before the mid-1970s, when technology made world-wide broadcasting possible, church spokesmen were discovering new and extensive areas for their electronics ministry. Television had by then become an established force of the greatest power in American life; preachers were learning how to use it. So quickly did they learn, as the next five chapters will suggest, that by 1980 the evangelism electronics empire had a total annual budget of some six hundred million dollars, with every sign indicating more growth to come.

Such phenomenal success has not been hailed with enthusiasm by some of the Christian leadership and laity in this nation. A substantial number of them are strongly, even bitterly, opposed to the present style and content of the ministry of the electronic church. They find its methods, its money raising, its format, indeed, virtually the full gamut of its operations, misleading, superficial, and potentially dangerous. One careful observer, Dr. Robert M. Liebert of State University of New York, Stony Brook, has called this opposition the beginnings of "a holy war" within American Christendom. He argued, "nothing less than the definition of Christianity is at stake in this holy war." [2] Other participants in electronics ministry have reacted in much the same way (*see Chapter 9*).

RADIO EVANGELISM

War or not, airwaves evangelism started quietly enough. On January 2, 1921, at the nation's first "full-fledged" radio station, KDKA, Pittsburgh, an evening worship service from Calvary Episcopal Church was broadcast. The program was limited to the traditional service, the only change being the presence of the radio engineers.[3] Radio itself became instantly popular in all areas of American life, not the least being evangelistic preaching. Early pioneers included Paul Radar of Chicago, George Pauler, Lois Crawford, and R. R. Brown, who created, in essence, radio congregations. By the mid 1930s, station managers, producers, and denominational leaders understood that a vast, loyal audience of listeners was out there waiting for about as much religious broadcasting as the airwaves could carry.[4]

Some stations responded with great quantity, until stations were "drowning one another in bedlam of squeaks, whistles, and disjointed words." [5] Congress moved to establish some order, equity, and stability by creating the Federal Radio Commission. Without prior experience for direction, it established some policies which in essence curbed rather than stabilized religious programming. But out of the confusion emerged the national celebrity-preacher system, led by such great evangelists as Walter A. Maier of *The Lutheran Hour* and Charles E. Fuller of *The Old-Fashioned Revival Hour*. Along with others, they created loyal followers with their regular weekly programs. In turn, other preachers built followings on more regional and local levels. By the end of World War II religious radio programming was an accepted and usually self-supporting ingredient in American religious life. It has remained a major force, reflecting in its variety the full range of the religious expressions of its audiences.[6]

THE TV BOOM

During the late 1930s, broadcasters started showing tiny, and by today's standards, amusing little gadgets called "television sets." Their technological improvement increased at high speed, and within 20 years television had become one of the most powerful inventions in communications history. One of its historians suggests that it greatly accelerated the broadcasting of information, leaping over the gulfs of time and place. It also restored face-to-face communication, something the telephone and radio could not do. Television helped eliminate differences among educated and uneducated, offering knowledge to anyone who could see, without access to formal centers of learning. Even more powerful was the fact that television "conveys a sense of immediacy and urgency"; it seems like real life. It redefines "reality" for the viewer.[7] And, in the early 1980s its uses were being expanded at an even more accelerated rate.

Since the celebrity-preacher format had worked well for radio, American church leaders involved in electronic ministry launched their television programs in the early 1950s with the same structure. Not knowing precisely why, they did know that having a brilliant, warm personality deliver the message brought enthusiastic approval from the viewers. Among the first giants was Bishop Fulton J. Sheen. Avoiding entertainment gimmicks used by television entertainers, he presented weekly 30-minute nondenominational homilies. His mail ran at about 6000 letters a day; he remained in television until 1966.

Following Sheen came another innovater, the Rev. Rex Humbard. He created what would become a widely imitated format of televising a weekly church service, this from Akron, Ohio, with the auditorium constructed to meet the technological needs of cameras, cables, and lighting.

Still another forerunner was Oral Roberts, first of the Pentecostal community, then later a Methodist, a university president, and by about 1960 a household word best known for his services of spiritual and physical healing. Such a ministry had long been practiced in Pentecostal churches. Roberts turned it into the hallmark of his national ministry. Millions of viewers faithfully supported his vigorous prayers, laying on of hands, and the testimonies of those claiming to be healed. Countless others concluded the Roberts ministry smacked too much of razzmatazz showmanship, unprovable scientific claims, and unaccounted-for financial collections.[8]

Finally, among the giants of the 1950s, Billy Graham and the *Hour of Decision* program came to be the pacesetter. Considered from the 1950s to the present by the annual newswire polls as "the most influential Protestant in America," Graham pursued his specialty, the altar-call, instant-conversion form of evangelism. He did preach, as did Sheen; he did have elements of a worship service, as did Humbard; he did talk about the glories of the born-again life, as did Roberts. Yet Graham's television ministry was one of a kind. Every telecast included his call to "leave your seats, walk down the aisles, come up in front here and give yourself to Jesus." Tens of thousands of people at his rallies followed the call, and millions of supporters wrote his headquarters with testimonies of their loyalty to his television ministry.[9]

Humbard, Roberts, and Graham continued their electronic ministry into the 1970s and early 1980s. Their success helped bring other preachers into the television ministry such as Robert Schuller, Jimmy Swaggart, Cecil Todd, and Morris Cerullo. Each of these carefully created his own kind of outreach, his own visible identity distinct from the others. That was in harmony with the theorists of television broadcasting at that time; overlapping or duplicating tended to confuse the viewers. Each of these leaders found enough support to continue with his individual ministry; they had mastered the challenges of broadcasting religious programs in a totally new medium.

THE NEW GENERATION OF
TV PREACHER

Yet their strengths would become their limitations. Their formats were locked in, their visibility was indelibly etched in the viewer's consciousness. That stability would become a limitation, starting in the mid 1970s when the "electronic church" as we know it came into national prominence. As we will see in the next four chapters, the pioneers would not find a shrinking audience; indeed their financial support would grow in those years. Rather they would discover that the lessons they had learned about effective television evangelism had been learned well by a younger set of preachers. Each of these would be willing to tell the Good News, to meet the needs of the viewers, in innovative ways beyond the stable formats of the early leaders.

Already by the early 1960s one of those later to become a dominant force, Pat Robertson, was carrying out a small television ministry in Portsmouth, Virginia. Growth was very slow until, quite without planning, an innovation came to the broadcaster. According to Robertson's vice-president, Stan Ditchfield,

> the Lord miraculously opened up "The 700 Club" concept to us in the mid-1960s. During a telethon, a viewer called in not to pledge but to ask for prayer. The pledgetaker prayed with her and something happened. Suddenly television was not the same anymore; people could call in and be prayed with immediately. TV had become a two-way, responsive medium.[10]

A second new feature of the budding electronic church was its flexibility in talking about events of current interest. Viewers did not have to wait until Sunday or a four-time-a-year program to hear a minister's interpretation of some current crisis; it was right there, every day. Of special interest to many viewers was the emphasis the television preachers placed on interpreting the times as the Last Days, the final judgments of God on an increasingly evil world. For those who tried to interpret the signs of the times, the electronic ministers offered daily guidance.

Thirdly, the new set of ministers discovered their ratings and their resources expanded enormously when they linked their ministries with traditional morality, conservative political programs, and vigorous patriotism. Viewers wanted to hear preachers declare that a specific moral situation was either right or wrong, that it was time to get back to the old verities of righteousness and self-reliance in legislation, and to celebrate proudly the fact that America, under God, was still his instrument for the world. Out of their personal convictions the electronic preachers grasped the national trend toward conservatism in politics, morality, and life-style. They heard from their viewers that the ministers in the pulpits were not saying what the audiences wanted to hear. The few mainline religious television programs being broadcast were generally unfulfilling to those who knew what a preacher should be talking about. When the new generation of television ministers stood up for those convictions, they broke down the locked-in identity roles of the earlier television preachers and tapped into a huge new audience.[11]

Next, by contrast to the pioneers, electronic preachers concentrated directly on meeting personal, immediate needs of the viewers. This was provided largely through counseling over the telephone those with doubts, fears, or prayer requests. By contrast to the local parish where only one minister (in an average congregation) was available to meet such needs, now viewers found 24-hour hot-line counselling available without appointments, with full anonymity, and with simple, direct answers to their calls. Neither the older television preachers or the local churches could compete with such personal services.

The new preachers, especially Robertson and Jim Bakker, were able to move beyond the pioneers also because they freely utilized entertainment techniques from secular television. They created an atmosphere of spontaneity, of surprise, of freedom from a fixed liturgy, of upbeat smiling hosts ready at any time to take up the most serious issues of the day. And, they did so with highly impressive technical proficiency. Theirs was not the familiar Sunday morning mainline religious panel show, with three speakers, and a plastic potted palm for a setting. They used the most sophisticated and advanced technology available in the electronics world.[12]

In summary, the new electronics preachers used several original ingredients to carry and keep themselves at the top. A viewer, either alone or with family or friends, has a choice over the kind of religious programs she or he can watch. They can feel good about staying at home watching a service. They can feel part of a national growing organization which has its priorities precisely defined. The viewer can thus avoid having to dress up to attend a service at the local congregation, with the possibility of an off-key choir, an average-to-mediocre sermon from a too-liberal or just-dull preacher, and can avoid the other small irritants endemic in a local congregation. Between 1975 and 1980, for a growing number of Americans the option of the electronic church has been irresistible.[13]

_____Four_____

Pat Robertson,
the *700 Club,*
and the Christian
Broadcasting Network

The story of the entrance of the electronic church into the New Christian Right, with its distinctive politics of moralism, is best told by focusing on its four leaders. Drawing on the new technology as well as the new religious and political climate of the 1970s, these preachers put together a unified message and launched programs which carried them to their positions of national power. They had competitors, but by 1980 the four most influential trend setters were Pat Robertson, Jim Bakker, Jerry Falwell, and James Robison. They alone could not have produced the New Christian Right; in turn, it would never have appeared without them.

Pat Robertson was the first of these ministers to use a television station for full-time ministry. He had reached that career by a roundabout path. The son of a United States Senator, Robertson used his Yale Law School degree in his first job with a Manhattan electronics firm. In 1956 he experienced a life-changing encounter with a Christian missionary. Robertson had a born-again conversion, enrolled at New York Biblical Seminary, and prepared for the ministry. He was ordained in the Southern Baptist Convention. With his wife and family, he spent the first years of ministry working in dilapidated sections of Brooklyn and Manhattan, a long way from the patrician Tidewater Virginia of his youth.

SIMPLE BEGINNINGS

In 1959 the Robertsons moved back to Virginia. There he purchased a run-down, virtually abandoned television station in Portsmouth. Robertson started the Christian Broadcasting Network (CBN), working for a year to prepare the station WYAH (*YAH* means "God" in Hebrew) for broadcasting. On October 1, 1961, the first show was beamed from this, the first television station licensed to broadcast primarily religious programs.

That show was not a success. "A man proclaimed the word of God from a crude wooden pulpit," the CBN description reads. "Behind him hung a faded gray curtain and a cardboard cross. The television signal was weak. The equipment broke down twice on the air. A film jammed in the projector." [1] The program signal carried to the edge of town.

Robertson persisted, short not of energy but of money. He studied regular television programming and decided to use the telethon fund raising format employed by the muscular dystrophy agencies. He projected a need of $7000 a month for expenses, so he appealed on the telethon for 700 people to pledge $10 each month—hence the name of his program, the *700 Club*.[2] Funds remained in short supply, so Robertson again studied commercial television. The CBN purchased and increased the power of a small radio station, WXRI, using it for ministry and for promoting the television station. In 1965 Robertson decided to bring expertise into the program. He hired a former manager of Billy Graham's television program as his director. He also hired Jim and Tammy Bakker, free-lance evangelists, to start a children's program for WYAH.

THE BREAKTHROUGH

For the next few years growth was slow. Then, quite unexpectedly came the major breakthrough of the shared prayer between a caller and a WYAH telephone correspondent. Robertson and his staff understood the potential audience and installed a 24 hour-a-day call-in telephone service; they trained volunteers for counselling those calling in. In addition to the calls, Robertson himself responded on camera to requests for healing. Having received that spiritual gift through the Pentecostal "Baptism in the Holy Spirit," he laid on hands for television viewers and he prayed for the sick as they called in. The viewers could see a 700 Club minister respond to their requests and announce that the specific ailment be cast out (the callers' names were not mentioned). In the past, Oral Roberts had conducted healing services on television. Robertson, however added the call-in ingredient, giving his televising a one-to-one closeness lacking in other video healing services. Robertson and his staff frequently explained the nature of the Pentecostal gifts; they themselves spoke in tongues and urged the viewers to pray to receive that gift. However, Robertson kept speaking in tongues off the broadcast. It was too complex, often "cornball or zany" to the uninformed in the audience.[3]

Now with an identity feature of its own, the *700 Club* program expanded more rapidly. The viewers responded enthusiastically to innovations such as interviewing celebrities, having upbeat, well rehearsed music, having a co-emcee, introducing discussion of current world events with specialists—in brief, following the format of talk shows such as Johnny Carson's. During these years the CBN technicians became more proficient, more aware of the ways in which lighting, staging, sound, and color could help give the program a high professional polish.

CRUSADING MORALISM

The seeds for the politics of moralism were planted early in Robertson's television ministry. Robertson and his announcers talked frequently about the "unprecedented moral decay" in America, created by "secular humanism" and sweeping over the populace. In Robertson's estimate, we were well along the way to abolishing any standards of time-proven morality from public or private life. Selfish indulgence in personal pleasure was the only goal for millions of Americans; the older stern dedication to hard work, virtue, and denial of instant gratification was fast departing the American shores.

To prove his case, Robertson used as evidence the growing feminist movement exemplified by the Equal Rights Amendment, which he found immoral. Further evidence was the increase of homosexuality, pornography, the number of illegitimate babies, and abortion "on demand." The *700 Club* preachers were evidently talking about those issues which local ministers avoided or watered down; the viewers liked what they found on their screens. The preachers also deplored the influence of liberal theology and sophisticated analyses of biblical texts. Finally, to Robertson the worst culprits of all were the national television networks, newspapers, and magazines peddling secular humanism, glorifying self-indulgence, and encouraging disrespect for traditional authority. With his born-again commitment, Robertson dedicated the CBN to fight all these enemies.[4] This was

34

something new in electronic evangelism; crusading moralism was building a loyal audience.

By 1976 the success of the revitalized ministry and the technological skills showed up in the growth statistics. By mid-year CBN owned and operated some 50 television and radio stations in various parts of the country. Robertson was a national celebrity in charismatic circles for his leadership in the annual "Jesus Festivals," outdoor rallies for youth. Usually attracting about 25,000 participants annually since their inception in 1973, the festivals were strongly Pentecostal. Robertson preached on receiving the gifts of tongues and conducted healings. In 1976, for instance, as he spoke "a stream of young people flowed to the platform to confirm they had been suddenly healed (of epilepsy, cancer of the uterus, a fracture). Several said their eyesight had been corrected, and they smashed their glasses. One youth said that he had been plagued by lust from the age 13 but was now delivered." [5] Obviously, Robertson was not responsible for such excesses. His presence at such rallies, however, gave the *700 Club* much of its unique identity, which continues to the present day.

RAPID GROWTH

In that same year, Robertson made his boldest move yet, one unprecedented in evangelistic circles. At Virginia Beach, Virginia, he broke ground for the construction of an elaborate "International Communications Center" for the CBN. It would be a complex of buildings for a variety of programs: electronics evangelism for full-time students, a new headquarters for the *700 Club*, an international counselling center, a round-the-clock prayer center, technology to broadcast the *700 Club* around the world and, eventually, a school of theology.

As it was planned, and as it has been developing, the CBN resembles a new denomination in American church life.

Rapid growth continued with the expanded facilities. New radio and television stations were added, programs were sent overseas, the buildings started taking shape at the headquarters, and the money kept coming. By 1978 Robertson could say, "Look out, CBS, NBC, and ABC. You're in for some stiff competition in the television news field." [6] Robertson was aiming, he said, for "the billion dollar category" of financial strength.[7] The goal was not an idle wish. By 1979 CBN was broadcasting its daily 90-minute program on 150 domestic and international stations, and over 1,800 cable systems. It enrolled 285,000 members (contributors), and announced a cash income of 54 million dollars for that year. Robertson sent out a monthly newsletter, *The Perspective* with additional personal insights in world and spiritual matters. In the newsletter Robertson spoke more about political issues than he did on the air. The CBN employed some 800 workers for its many programs; it had 12,000 volunteers at 83 prayer and counselling centers; in that year they received 1.4 million telephone calls.[8]

CBN went on to purchase four full-time religious programming television stations. By mid-1980 the International Center at Virginia Beach was completed, attracting large numbers of visitors. CBN also started a ministry "Operation Blessing," which gave food, clothing, and other necessities to needy recipients in several cities. Throughout all this expansion, Robertson kept CBN in every way independent from any denominational affiliation or accountability.

The money, which kept increasing, made the growth possible; the CBN fund raisers solicited it with a variety of methods. The telethons continued; direct mail appeals from computerized lists increased in size; spin-offs such as tapes, books, and regional rallies brought additional funds. Beyond this, Robertson utilized what he called "Kingdom Principles." These were, in essence, requests for funds from the viewers. They were informed that if they would write down "Seven Lifetime Prayer Requests" and send them, along with $100, to CBN, the requester's name would be placed on microfilm. That film, including the names of all such supporters, would be placed in a pillar. There the seven requests would be engulfed by 24-hour-a-day prayer. At various times Robertson would pray at the pillar. Kneeling he would ask for miraculous intervention: "Heal cancers, right now. Mend broken homes now. Cure madness now. Thank you Jesus, thank you, Lord. Supply financial needs right now, in the name of Jesus. Thank you, Lord." [9]

With so successful a career, Robertson had opened a field for ministry undreamed of only two decades ago. Today he stands as the pacesetter. Other evangelists, however, were already at work in the same vineyard.

Five

Jim Bakker
and the *PTL Club*

Second to Robertson in age and experience, but not in influence or innovation, is Jim Bakker, head of the *PTL Club* ("Praise the Lord," "People That Love"). Were the two leaders not so different in physical appearance and television presence, a new viewer of both shows would have considerable difficulty in keeping the two apart. Similarities are evident in their skillful use of television technology, their fund raising, emphasis on healing, providing media training for aspiring broadcasters, and appealing to the same traditional code of morality—and therefore to the same audience. But so large has that audience grown since 1975 that more than enough room exists for both programs. Hence, the two furnished ample broadcasting time for their contributions to the politics of moralism; viewers in any part of the country by 1980 could invariably find one of the two, and often both on a daily basis.[1]

Despite the similarities, the contrasts between Robertson and Bakker have always been evident. Bakker was reared in Muskegon, Michigan, where his father was employed as a machinist. In contrast to Robertson's decision for ministry later in life, Bakker knew early that he was going to be a preacher. His personal faith was shaped during a severe emotional crisis; when driving an automobile Bakker accidently struck a young boy. Eventually the patient recovered, helped, Bakker believes, by the prayers for supernatural healing from him and his friends.[2] That event became a landmark in Bakker's thought—a sign that believers should expect divine healing.

In his late teens Bakker enrolled in North Central Bible College in Minneapolis, there receiving the Pentecostal baptism in the Holy Spirit. In September, 1960, he met Tammy Faye LaValley. They became engaged, then married, knowing the school's prohibition against student marriages. They resigned before graduation and became full-time free-lance evangelists.

Together on the road, the pair travelled "as a gospel team, sleeping in pastors' bedrooms, cheap motel rooms, dusty church attics, accepting whatever meager 'love offering' their host church offered."[3]

Unlike the other electronic preachers, *PTL Club* gives Tammy Bakker a major role as co-host, the only woman to be so prominent in electronics evangelism. She had learned her public presence well during the years on the road. Secondly, Bakker states in his autobiography that during the lean times he came to trust in miraculous, supernatural responses from God to the Bakkers' specific needs; he describes 55 events when God answered their requests for material needs or for healing. The confidence underpins the *PTL* format today.

BEGINNING WITH ROBERTSON

In 1965 the Bakkers decided they should enter television evangelism with a talk show. Through a friend they heard of Robertson's work in Virginia. They talked with him at some length, deciding on a partnership in which the Bakkers would do the children's program and a late-night talk show. The Bakker's fortunes rose and fell with those of Robertson; despite the slow start, Bakker stayed with CBN. "I was fully committed to Christian television," he said.[4]

That commitment was tested over the next few years. When asked by Robertson, Bakker added radio broadcasting to his work at CBN. One night, however, he refused to take an additional radio shift. Robertson and he talked it over, and, in Bakker's explanation, "Pat finally said, 'We've established a chain of command here, and you've broken it.'" Bakker was given the options of resigning or paying a $100 fine. Bakker refused both; Robertson waited a week, then paid the fine himself, and more normal relations returned.

The final strain came on November 8, 1972. In his own words Bakker says,

> The Lord spoke to me *"I want you to resign your job at CBN today."* I didn't like the idea much. I had an expensive house to continue paying for, and without a regular paycheck, I would quickly lose it, as well as my automobile. "God, I'll make a deal with You," I said, foolishly trying to bargain with the Lord. "You sell my house, and then I'll resign the job." *"No,"* he answered. *"You must resign first and then I will sell your house."*

That day Bakker told Robertson, "God has told me to leave CBN." Robertson said he couldn't "argue with that." After seven years Bakker and Robertson were no longer working together.[5]

Other observers have added further explanations to

the resignation. Bakker apparently objected to Robertson's Calvinistic predestination view of the relationship between God and man; Bakker held to an Arminian belief in free will. In public the two men have paid tribute to each other, Robertson pointing out that the *PTL Club* used "variations on format and concepts which we developed in the early days," while Bakker lists Robertson as one person to whom his autobiography was dedicated. The two have not participated on each other's programs; by 1978 the *Christian Century* reported "growing conflict" and "strained relations" between the two. Whatever the final explanation, Bakker quickly started his own program. Within five years, as an independent he would reach the top.[6]

ON THEIR OWN

His ascent started with the Bakkers moving to Southern California to explore the market for a religious television network there. They syndicated some ideas and moved to North Carolina in 1973 with hopes of having their own operations. After a slow start, during which the viewing audience evaluated this new kind of evangelism, the *PTL Club* found enough supporters to keep on the air. Then, in a short time, the format of telephone counselling, talk shows, healing services, upbeat entertainment, and moralistic preaching took hold.

In the same year that Robertson started his new center, 1976, Bakker announced plans for the *PTL* complex near Charlotte. Named "Heritage Village," it embraced some 25 acres, with the architecture for the proposed headquarters building modeled after Bruton Parish Church of colonial Williamsburg, Virginia. The original costs for the Village came to two million dollars; Bakker collected it by accepting pledges as well as cash deposits. Additional buildings would include a college, a communications school for electronic evangelism, recreational facilities, and the best television and electronic equipment available anywhere.[7]

Apparently the most popular feature with the viewers was the attention given to healing, Pentecostal style. One observer noted:

> Bakker, attired in an egg-blue suit, standing against a velvet background begins quietly: "There is a prostate gland condition that God is healing right now . . . there is a spinal condition, perhaps a missing disc that is being restored . . . someone to my left has a kidney ailment . . . there are growths and in the name of Jesus those growths are gone . . . you will not need surgery . . . there is something that goes into the marrow of the bone, maybe it's leukemia . . . the Lord is healing it." [8]

Requests for healing came from the viewers to the telephone operators. The operators had in front of their phones computer forms which listed ailments alphabetically, starting with arthritis. In other boxes near the phones each operator had on cards lists of major emotional and spiritual crises. When a viewer called in one of these, the operator would write it down, send it to Bakker, and then counsel with the caller. Most of the time the answers were appropriate Bible verses crossindexed to meet the specific needs of the viewer. Thus the persons calling in could have Scripture addressed to their specific requests, as well as having someone talk or pray with them at that moment. On occasion Bakker would ask viewers to call in and give testimonials of what had happened to them after they had made known their requests to *PTL*. Calls came in, and Bakker told the viewers of the miracles at work. It was all happening on the screen where everyone could see and hear.[9]

In addition to the healings, Bakker's generous use of polished singers, orchestras, celebrity speakers, and vigorous preaching helped keep *PTL* growing. The statistics show the trend. From 46 in 1975, the total number of television stations carrying the daily program reached 197 by 1978, including 14 overseas outlets and 123 cable networks.[10] By mid-summer, 1979, the annual revenue was nearing 45 million dollars (it went over 52 million in 1980). In 1979 PTL employed 700 workers, and contributors for the Club reached over 700,000.[11]

OVERCOMING PROBLEMS

For a while such growth was seriously threatened when the Internal Revenue Service asked if the *PTL* was sending designated funds to their proper destinations. The IRS suspected that some money, designated for overseas missions, was being spent elsewhere. That raised doubts in the minds of contractors for Heritage Village, some of whom demanded instant cash payment out of fear the *PTL* treasury was running dry. A local newspaper, *The Charlotte Observer*, noted these problems and pointed out that the *PTL* accounting procedures were not standard in form, making any outside auditing difficult. The Federal Communications Commission decided to look directly at *PTL* records. Bakker refused their order, claiming that churches were exempt from that kind of government inspection. After over two years of legal maneuverings, testimony, court proceedings, and fund appeals, *PTL* was able to pay off its construction debts, improve its accounting procedures, and keep the IRS away from its records.[12]

By the end of 1980 Bakker could point to the smooth running of a many-sided program, all created in just over six years. At Heritage Center a campground and recreational facilities were usually filled with visitors, mostly vacationers coming to see *PTL* for themselves. The satellite network brought 24-hour-a-day religious programming to cooperating American and 40 overseas *PTL* programs. Bakker received the full endorsement of such old-timers as Rex Humbard and Oral Roberts. At the dedication of the facilities in 1980, Rev. Bob Maddox, President Carter's White House religious adviser, spoke with personal congratulations from the president. The counselling service grew; in 1979 it answered some 478,000 calls and, using some 3000 ministers, organized programs to get the callers to join local churches. To train students in electronics evangelism, the School of Communication was started, rivaling that of the CBN. Finally, considerable gifts of money and supplies were sent from Charlotte to refugees and displaced persons in Southeast Asia.[13]

Once he was head of his own organization, Bakker learned his lessons well and added some important features of his own. Fully in accord with Robertson on Pentecostal faith, Bakker placed alongside a "health-and-wealth theology." To him the Christian life meant praying, expecting God to meet your needs. Positive thinking that God would do that was essential to the prayer being answered. God wanted his people to be healthy, to prosper, to thrive in this world. So long as believers accepted that, they knew, in one of Bakker's favorite phrases, "The Lord is on your side." [14]

In early 1981 the *PTL* stands alongside the *700 Club* as a major voice, adding money, outreach, and innovation to electronic evangelism. During the growth years Bakker prepared linkages to the politics of moralism by preaching on the sins of pornography, child abuse, narcotics, marital infidelity, abortion, homosexuality—the list that would become the domain of the New Christian Right. To these questions, and to the personal needs of the viewers, he presents a smiling, happy image and a set of appealing, uncomplicated answers. The audience continues to grow.

Six

Jerry Falwell and
The Old-Time Gospel Hour

Because the electronic church has such growth potential for evangelists, it attracts and rewards those willing to go beyond traditional forms of outreach. Nowhere is this more evident than in the career of Jerry Falwell, of Lynchburg, Virginia, pastor of Thomas Road Baptist Church and featured speaker for *The Old-Time Gospel Hour* television program. In his 25 years of ministry he has built a reputation and a following which command strong national attention. His voice is among the most powerful on the politics of moralism; his leadership places him squarely at the head of the New Christian Right.

Like Bakker, Falwell grew up in a simple, small-town environment. Born as a twin in 1933 in Lynchburg, he would make his home town the base for his electronics empire. He chose mechanical engineering for his major in Lynchburg College. In his late teens he started listening regularly to one of the giants of radio preaching, Charles E. Fuller on *The Old-Fashioned Revival Hour*. One Sunday evening at a local Baptist church in 1952 Falwell heard the preacher deliver a sermon much like those of Fuller. When the altar call was made, Falwell came forward. He dates this as his born-again moment of conversion. Two months later he decided to enter the full-time ministry.[1] After two years at Lynchburg College, Falwell completed his formal education with two more years at Baptist Bible College in Springfield, Missouri.

THE BEGINNINGS

Following his ordination he returned to Lynchburg. There in June, 1956 with a nucleus of 35 adults, he founded Thomas Road Baptist Church. From there to the prominence achieved by the summer of 1980, with his portrait on the cover of *Newsweek* (Sept. 15, 1980) he found means and energies to expand his ministry. As early as 1956 he started a local television program and a daily 30-minute radio show. He also preached and led prayer meetings in cities within a two-hundred-mile radius of Lynchburg.

His first priority during the early years was to the local parish. Falwell's several talents—fund raiser, preacher, builder—were soon translated into rapid membership growth. Within two decades Thomas Road Baptist showed a membership of 15,000, "one of the nation's five largest churches." [2] This expansion included a larger church auditorium, additional education buildings, and, in 1971 the start of a college. First known as Lynchburg Baptist, it later became Liberty Baptist College and something of a showcase for the Falwell ministry. After a slow beginning, the school expanded rapidly during "the boom years of the evangelicals," the mid 1970s. Falwell also found the resources and expertise to add a Bible institute, seminary, and academy.[3]

With all this growth, the centerpiece remained the

weekly national television program, *The Old-Time Gospel Hour*. Falwell remained with the format of televising a regular church service, rather than joining Robertson and Bakker in daily shows. Also, in contrast to them, Falwell consistently preached a theology of traditional fundamentalist doctrine. As his empire grew, Falwell added more staff and spent more time travelling across the country preaching to audiences familiar with his television program. He was, by the late 1970s, a national celebrity.[4]

Falwell organized his support in a way distinctive from the CBN and *PTL*. Viewers have four different subdivisions from which they can choose to support the programs. The first is known as "Faith Partners," a membership requiring a pledge of $10 a month to the television program. Second is the "I Love America Club," with contributors sending in $12 a month to battle, in Falwell's words, "the moral cancers" facing America. Next is the Liberty Missionary Society, to which donations are made for overseas evangelism. Finally, Falwell has the "Liberty Mountain Scholar Share," asking for donations to support Liberty Baptist College. The funds did come in. By mid-1980, being on 373 television stations, claiming an audience of 25 million viewers, the total operation was grossing 56 million dollars annually.[5]

PREPARING FOR ARMAGEDDON

Falwell's fundamentalism sets him near to the teachings of the other television preachers, including the pioneers. Like them, he has studied the television audiences and knows those themes and programs to which they will respond. He avoids the *PTL* "health and wealth" position, as well as Robertson's frequent illustrated lectures on international politics. At the core for Falwell, indeed the key to his ministry, is his conviction on the Bible. It "is indeed the inerrant Word of God of the living God. The Bible is absolutely infallible, without error in all matters pertaining to faith and practice, as well as in areas such as geography, science, history, etc." [6] From this flows the acceptance of the doctrines of the virgin birth of Christ, the substitutionary atonement, the physical resurrection and ascension and a no compromise commitment to the "Pre-Tribulation Rapture." [7]

This premillennial position is basically also that of the other three leading electronic preachers. As Falwell explains it, when Christ returns to rule on earth for the millennium, his appearance will be preceded by seven years of the Tribulation, in which the Anti-Christ will arise, Russia will invade Israel, and worldwide persecution of Christians will occur. Then the Battle of Armageddon will be fought, in which Christ and his legions will defeat Satan and his forces; Christ will reign bodily over the earth for 1000 years, after which the final Judgment will be held. All of this becomes crucial in electronic preaching because the fundamentalist consensus is that the world may well be nearing the End Times right now. Falwell suggests the Christian church will exist for 2000 years; and it has already used up 1980 of those. Hence, as he writes "in these last days" the citizens of the world are entering the 1980s, "The Decade of Destiny." [8]

For evidence on this, so vital a matter to his ministry, Falwell produces what to him are documented proofs of the imminence of the Last Days. These include wars and rumors of wars, extreme materialism, departure from the Christian faith by millions, overpopulation, lawlessness, an increase in knowledge, intense demonic activity, the unification of the mainline church groups (i.e., the National and World Councils of Churches, Vatican II), recent developments in Russia and in Israel, and finally "the absence of dynamic leadership."[9] Such absence has helped convince the television preachers that they must take up the slack and prepare believers for the final days; to them the 1980 election was not too early an entry point. In brief, the New Christian Right was writing out its agenda, and Falwell furnished much of the impetus. His role in "Moral Majority" will be explored in Chapter 11.

SIGNIFICANT DIFFERENCES

United as they are on the End Times, the electronic preachers divide sharply over one of the major ingredients in the *PTL* and *700 Club,* Pentecostal healing. Falwell, like many fundamentalists, avoids healing services. The statement of doctrine for the Lynchburg complex of schools reads:

> One danger today is more emphasis is placed on the baptism of the Holy Spirit, the gifts of the Spirit and speaking in tongues than is placed on Jesus Christ and the blood He shed so lost souls might be saved. The Holy Spirit must glorify Christ and not gifts or His own power (John 16:14). We do not believe in the showy healing meetings that are being held in the name of the Lord today. If you check into the practices of the so-called faith healers, you would find only certain ones are allowed to come forward for healing, many are not cured (sometimes many are not even sick) and many times people are planted in the audience to feign certain ailments so it can appear they have been healed.[10]

Nowhere in the Lynchburg-Falwell complex are there exhortations to seek the baptism in the Holy Spirit or any of the traditional Pentecostal gifts.

Another difference between Falwell and the others is his policy of being on national television for only one hour a week. This means *The Old-Time Gospel Hour* cannot have the flexibility, adaptability (it is taped four weeks in advance) and instant up-to-date quality of *PTL* or *700 Club*. Instead Falwell has chosen to continue with his many personal appearances, especially leading the Liberty Bible College students across the nation in a stage presentation, *I Love America*. Beyond that he supervises the several programs at home, keeps up with his radio Bible studies, and supervises planning for expansion.[11]

Given these differences among the leaders, it is necessary to point out that substantial agreement among them is abundant. They all are steadily improving the technical quality of their broadcasting; they have large, effective staffs, but keep their own names at the center of their programs for identification and to hold the loyalty of supporters. They all feature smiling faces, upbeat sounds, promises of success and redemption. All unabashedly proclaim America as the most Christian nation on earth, God's instrument to do his will. All utilize the traditional symbols of America's civil religion (the flag, the patriotic monuments, the famous buildings in Washington, D.C.) as icons of loyalty to the nation. All three condemn secular humanism and political liberalism as satanic threats to America; all three call for revival now. Such sources feed directly into the politics of moralism.

Seven

James Robison
and the
Evangelism Association

Falwell's mushrooming success has attracted talented imitators, just as Bakker followed in Robertson's path. The most influential electronic pulpiteer whose ministry closely parallels that of Falwell is the Reverend James Robison of Fort Worth, Texas. His rise to prominence in the last four years places him squarely among the national leaders in the New Christian Right; his theology and ethics make him as important a spokesman as the other three for the politics of moralism. What he lacks, compared to that trio, is a multi-sided, million-dollar-a-week program. However, as the New Right expands at the outset of the '80s, Robison is well on the way to catching up with his fellow electronic evangelists.

Like Bakker and Falwell, Robison had a childhood marked by hardship and lack of educational opportunity. In fact, Robison's early years were the most difficult of all. He was born in a charity ward of a Houston hospital in 1943 to an alcoholic mother abandoned by her husband. Having been refused an abortion by a local doctor, she carried the baby to term, then placed a newspaper ad asking someone to provide a home for the newborn. The Rev. and Mrs. H. D. Hale of Pasadena, Texas gave James a home until his mother reclaimed him five years later. The boy spent ten years with her in Augustine, Texas, then returned to the Hales and finished high school.

THE YOUNG PREACHERS

In his fifteenth year Robison answered an altar call at Memorial Baptist Church during a local revival. That led him to decide on a full-time career in the ministry, which he began by enrolling at East Texas Baptist College in Marshall. He started conducting revivals when still a first-year student. Within a few months observers noted his flair for vigorous evangelistic preaching. By the age of 19 he had received some 1000 invitations to conduct crusades in 27 states.[1]

After college and ordination Robison devoted full time to evangelism. Best known in the Southwest, he worked in the early '70s to expand his outreach towards a national audience. Like Falwell, he recognized the potential for electronic evangelism and started his own weekly show. By word of mouth and by energetic promotion through cooperating local clergy, Robison rapidly started adding new stations to his network. He impressed his viewers as one who spoke with strong conviction, who had a nimble grasp on using appropriate biblical proof texts, and an intuitive grasp for the interests of his audiences. Alongside his revivals and television Robison, far more than the other three leaders, produced a large number of tracts following up on his television and one-night preaching missions. Within the framework of the successful electronic preachers, he was finding his strengths and unique identity; the audiences responded with contributions.

THE MORALISM CONNECTION

These qualities alone, however, would not have carried him to the position of national leadership he now commands. During 1978 and 1979 Robison started giving increasing time and enthusiasm in his preaching and writing to public morality—to the major issues the New Christian Right would use as their "moral report cards" by which to evaluate the voting records of national lawmakers. This was something of a calculated risk for the young Texan, since he had always preached before in more traditional revivalist terms.

Robison, however, carried through his innovations, convinced that America was in a state of moral collapse. Earlier than any of the other three spokesmen, he started preaching that no longer could fundamentalists and evangelicals rely on saving America by individual conversions. Now, Robison stated, the real Christians must take hold of the political structures of the nation to save not only this country, but Christianity itself. That turn-around—from private to public displays of political morality—staked out for Robison the identity he would carry to the head of the movement.[2]

Robison had personal reasons for launching what would be the New Christian Right, as well as those from his doctrinal convictions. One of his Sunday morning stations was in Dallas. The station suddenly cancelled his program after he had preached that homosexuality was "an abomination in the eyes of God." The station argued that his show presented only one side of certain problems, while the Federal Communications Act, with its fairness doctrine, required equal time. Robison fought back, catching national attention not only over the homosexuality issue (much in the news at the time with the activities of Anita Bryant) but because of his slogan

54

"Freedom of speech, freedom to preach." The Dallas station later reinstated the program. Robison chose to press his advantage:

> If you can't preach that a man having sex with another man is against biblical morality without losing your freedom of speech, something is wrong.[3]

He well understood the backlash of American opinion against not only gay rights, but against the ERA, abortion, the ban on religious exercises in public schools, and fear that the United States was falling behind in the arms race with the Soviet Union. Robison started talking about those issues on television and in his crusades; his support increased with lightning speed. In July, 1980, the James Robison Evangelistic Association reached a wide national audience with a television special, *Wake Up America: We Are All Hostages*. The special contained the New Christian Right indictment of moral decay in this nation.

Robison now had enough money to expand his headquarters. Working out of Fort Worth, employing 150 workers, with a budget of 11 million dollars in 1980, he was finding an audience ready to hear more and give more. He had explored the potential of the mass media, and he had turned it into a growth enterprise.[4]

By the spring of 1980 his voice was recognized and respected enough in New Christian Right circles to give him a national office. He became vice-president of the Religious Roundtable and chairman of the National Prayer Committee, interested primarily in placing religious exercises in public schools. This was the reward for years of work as an independent revivalist, operating outside the structure of an established denomination. But for him the efforts were worth the contest. He had thought of the future:

> I'm going to be misunderstood a lot, but I'd like you to understand this. . . . I know the gifts that seemingly God's bestowed on me. I want you to understand why I do what I do. I don't move the way I do because I'm trying to find a popular course, a course that leads to material comfort. . . . I believe I could be elected to virtually any office in this land politically, but it's not what God's called me to do. God's called me to stand up before and do major spiritual surgery at the risk of my own life and even the love of the people toward me.[5]

He was referring to the fact his ministry, as he saw it, was to fundamentalists and evangelicals. He felt called to convince them that the greatest sin they were committing was in being apathetic towards the moral-political issues of the day. He startled more than a few of his listeners when he proclaimed it was not communists, not the political candidates. "It's you—far more than the politicians—who plague this country right now. Your attitude toward your fellow man is determined by your attitude toward God, and we have humanistic socialistic ideas now because we've gotten our eyes off God." [6] He called for direct political action, for "God's people to come out of the closets, out of the churches and change America." Shortly after the Republican national convention, Robison stated to a crowd, "A lot of people are disappointed in Reagan's vice-presidential choice. . . . You don't need to sit here and look at your politicians and expect them to do right when you haven't done right." "God's people," he exhorted, should not give up because George Bush was named for the vice-presidency; that was no reason to quit politics. His audience responded with prolonged applause.[7]

That kind of oratory, leadership, and energy are the major reasons for Robison's success. More bluntly than the other three leaders, he injects moralism by political action into his preaching. To some observers his style is needlessly abrasive; to others, he seems like an incarnated miracle. In contrast to Falwell, Robison has avoided a no-compromise position on charismatic healing, but joins the other three in adhering to a pre-tribulation rapture eschatology.

If any change in the positions of these four celebrities occurs in the near future, it is likely that Robison will move higher. He knows his heavy emphasis on politics is in sharp contrast with the "health and wealth" of some of his competitors. He is willing to make the risk. With his unique style, some 20 years of experience, a firm grasp on audience expectations and dynamics, and an up-and-doing personality, Robison stands early in 1981 on the verge of major national power which would slip only if "the politics of moralism" declined—like "the politics of doomsday" a decade ago.

Eight

Can the Good News Be Televised?: The Controversy Over the Electronic Church

The remarkable growth of electronic evangelism is symptomatic of powerful, but as yet not precisely definable, new trends in American religious and political life. Millions of Americans have already indicated they approve this expression of the Christian faith by their contributions and their use of the services of the electronic churches. As suggested, large new denominations may well appear within a few years, nurtured by the manner in which the leaders have adapted their message to this rapidly changing form of communication.

At the same time, the message and the methods of the television preachers have already generated strong criticism from church leaders and scholars. Even before the electronic pulpiteers became involved in the New Christian Right, their programs were meeting with considerable resistance from a variety of critics.

The criticisms embrace several different themes. The most important are these: (1) television itself creates a misleading, if not false, understanding of religious reality; (2) electronic-church theology is superficial; (3) television preachers draw both money and parishioners away from neighborhood congregations; (4) electronic evangelism concentrates too heavily on entertainment and oversimplification; and (5) several of its methods, which shape its message, are not clearly different from those of the secular world. By discussing these criticisms in this chapter, I am not necessarily agreeing with them; my effort throughout is to explore as carefully as possible what the New Christian Right is doing in American life.

SELLING JESUS

The most searching and debatable objection to electronic evangelism has been made by Virginia Stem Owens in her book *The Total Image: Or Selling Jesus in the Modern Age.*[1] She argues, first, that television exists to sell a product. The "best technique for selling is to paint for the customer a total picture of the kind of person he would like to be, and then make him believe your product is a necessary part of that picture."[2] The electronic preachers have adopted this approach. To Owens, rather than put *Christ* on the screen and thus limit the potential market, they place *people*, witnessing to the blessings of their born-again lives. That creates a profound misrepresentation. Accepting the image on the screen rather than the reality of daily religious life, "an unbeliever would not have an inkling that the original pattern these people profess to imitate was a vagrant celibate whose own seminar on happiness elevated the mourning meek rather than the smiling success."[3]

Electronic evangelism omits the failures; it has no time to explain ambiguity; it focuses exclusively on success, blessings, and happiness. To Owens, the camera cannot capture the reality of the Christian life in all of its complexity.

She continues by arguing that the television media

limits and even changes the viewer's perception of reality. It cannot probe the elements of silence, hiddenness, and mystery inherent in religious faith. In its determination to distract from anxiety, boredom, and isolation, television presents a false gospel. The media simply is not the real thing, hence it "perverts our reception of grace." [4] Television, Owen states, alters "the allegiance of the imagination, the very perception of reality." It gives "the illusion of access to God, or in the absence of God, to ultimate reality." [5]

Owens concludes with her alternative. Christians must continually judge and discriminate among the competing cultural values they encounter. The Kingdom of God, the Good News, is never found in a set of cultural values, but can be experienced and known in silence, hiddenness, and mystery. Religious faith is best nurtured within the local congregation with total presence and participation by real people conducting real worship or study corporately.[6] There the gospel cannot be condensed, simplified, or packaged, just as in the ministry of Jesus (Owens says that Jesus responded differently to each seeker without planned formulas). She summarizes, "a person, whether human or divine, cannot be known—as a person rather than an image—except by immediate presence. If we want to project an image, either of Christians or the church, we can do that by means of television, magazines, books, billboards, movies, bumper stickers, buttons, records, and posters. If we want people to know Christ, we must be there face to face, bearing Christ with us." [7]

In a similar vein, William F. Fore suggests that television is a window on the world which by its nature "filters and changes the reality it mediates." Television uses myth, symbol, image, and fantasy, thus distorting or even eliminating the strength of the local parish where people regularly come together on a face-to-face basis. Television messages, Fore claims, are those which the audience *wants* to hear, not necessarily the message of a God who requires justice, humility, and love.[8]

SUPERFICIAL THEOLOGY?

A second cluster of commentators believe television can be a meaningful way to tell the story, but the story they have heard so far is to them weak and superficial. Their criticisms thus are best understood as attempts to make the Good News strong and compelling. In early 1980 a comprehensive theological evaluation reached the public at a conference of leaders in religious communications, including some prominent electronic preachers.[9] The author was Fr. Richard P. McBrien, a professor at Boston College; his remarks are largely representative of others pursuing the same themes. He argues, first, the electronic church is really no "church" at all because the observer or participant finds no confession of faith "ratified in Baptism, the Eucharist, or Lord's Supper, and other sacraments" and no "sense of fellowship within the group . . . a common awareness of the call to become a community." To be sure, McBrien points out, several elements of an authentic church do exist in electronic evangelism—biblical preaching, a confession that Jesus is Lord, a clear standard of morality based on the Scriptures, and specific formal ministries at work.[10]

Yet, the theology is superficial. Its proclamation of the Good News is too narrow because the Christian proclamation must always place this life and world under the judgment of the Kingdom of God. That judgment must extend to one's personal conscience, as well as "those of governments, corporations, and institutions of every significant kind." McBrien does not hear this from the electronic preachers.[11] Moving to his major concern, the

61

theologian argues that the church does its evangelism by proclaiming that Jesus is Lord and measuring "the world and even the Christian community itself by the standards of the Kingdom." Any constriction of that evangelization in any form or by any communicator of the gospel fails to carry out the great commission.[12]

To date, McBrien suggests, television preachers have failed to explore the full content of the Christian message, especially the redemptive work of Christ, his life and ministry, his death, resurrection, and exaltation.

Such Christ-centered proclamation appears, he concludes, when the full authority of the word of God serves as the foundation for the proclamation. McBrien examines the electronic church understanding of biblical authority and finds it superficial. It simply leaves too many questions unanswered: "Does the New Testament give us the very words of Jesus? How do we know which are the authentic teachings of Jesus and which are not? How was the New Testament put together? What process was underway between the time Jesus died and rose and the time the books of the New Testament were finally edited? Which literary forms were employed in piecing the various elements of the tradition together? How does this pluralism of literary form affect our interpretation of the finished product? Who, indeed, interprets the Bible as we have it? Is its meaning self-evident? If so, why do we need anyone to preach to those who are already Christian?" [13]

McBrien concludes that since the television pulpiteers consider the Bible as a "self-sufficient authority for determining the content and meaning of the word of God, it begs the kinds of questions" he has raised. From such a position, the electronic preachers may offer answers which are so divisive that Christians will find resolution among them impossible.[14]

THE INVISIBLE RELIGION

A third, more practical evaluation is that the electronic church draws away both resources and parishioners from the local congregation. Martin E. Marty offers an explanation of why this occurs:

> Last Saturday night Mr. and Mrs. Invisible Religion got their jollies from the ruffled-shirted, pink-tuxedoed men and the high-coiffured, low-necklined celebrity women who talk about themselves under the guise of Born-Again autobiographies. Sunday morning the watchers get their jollies as Holy Ghost entertainers caress microphones among spurting fountains and a highly professional charismatic (in two senses) leader entertains them. Are they to turn off that very set and then make their way down the block to a congregation of real believers, sinners, offkey choirs, and sweaty and homely people who need them, people they do not like but are supposed to love, ordinary pastors who preach grace along with calls to discipleship, pleas for stewardship that do not come well-oiled? Well, hardly ever.[15]

In addition to keeping people at home, the electronic church is charged with depriving local parishes of much-needed revenue. In the past decade most mainline churches have undergone serious financial decline. Some of the blame, its leaders charge, rests with the television preachers who are by early 1981 each bringing in over a million dollars a week. By response, CBN officials point to studies they have made showing that "for every dollar contributed by CBN supporters to its ministry, four were contributed to the local church and other ministries." Further, another CBN study shows that 34 percent of its members state they became more involved in the local church as the result of watching the program; two percent said they became less involved.[16]

Without hard data, the correlation between mainline decline and television growth is difficult to prove. Professor Jeffrey Hadden suggests that the electronic church reaches not mainliners who cross over but lapsed or drop-out fundamentalists and evangelicals who had left their original churches, for whatever reasons, and now are turning to the electronic organization. These drop-outs reject the kind of religious broadcasting mainline denominations offer, but support the authoritative moral-istic programs on the screen. Their numbers are so large, Hadden suggests, that the comparatively small amounts each individual contributes can sustain the vast empires of Robertson, Bakker, Falwell, and Robison.[17]

CHRISTIAN SHOW BIZ

Next, considerable comment has been made on the tendency of the electronic church to entertain rather than edify, to oversimplify rather than challenge. Television has to keep the action moving quickly to hold the viewer's attention. It has time limits, forcing it to over-simplify or overdramatize complex issues. The viewers are less inclined to reflect on those demands of the faith which are rigorous and unflattering. Rather they "are more naturally inclined to that religious performance which impresses us with its spectacular character. The electronic church gives the audiences what they want, according to these critics.[18] Since it is flexible it can adjust quickly to new audience demands, while the local parish holds on to its familiar, traditional programs. The viewers who watch the electronic pulpiteers are pleased with what they see; they are entertained, they identify personally with the celebrities, they appreciate the telephone counselling, they respond favorably to these programs' sense of liveliness; the church down the street could not match them.[19]

Criticism emerges also from within evangelical ranks. The editors of *Eternity* magazine express serious doubts about "Christian Show Biz." A writer for the journal defined four problems with this form of ministry. First is the danger of exploitation. Often, well known entertainers were converted and quickly used by the electronic entrepreneurs before they had become firmly rooted in their born-again lives. A second problem has been that of excess and extravagance. Critics have asked if all the finery, all the posh trappings were necessary. The trappings created an atmosphere of "Christian entertainment becoming clubby and elitist for Christian 'beautiful people.'" Third was the issue of "going Hollywood," the temptation to have a first-rate technological and entertainment production which did not place the simple Good News at its center. Finally there have been the tensions among electronic evangelists over competition. They know the audiences are there, the resources are there, the power is there. The extent to cooperation among the leaders to date has not been impressive. Instead, programs became centered around personalities who wanted to protect and advance their programs with, at times, a lack of "humility before God." [20]

WORLDLY MARKETING

Finally, the pacesetters are brought to task by some for using secular methods of fund raising and advertising, regarding their message as a commodity. The critics say that the proclamation must stand under the judgment of God, rather than claiming, in Jim Bakker's phrase, "We have a better product than soap or automobiles. We have eternal life." [21] Other defenses of electronic promotion argue, "Aren't Christians in the business of selling, retailing the greatest product in the world? If so, why *shouldn't* Jesus Christ be promoted and marketed effectively?" [22] To that, another evangelical critic replies, using John 6:44: "No man can come to me except the Father which has sent me draws him." According to this critic, "gospel hucksterism" can only fail. Contemporary marketing techniques ignore the scandal, the stumbling block, the downright foolishness of the Christian faith. The programs raise money so they can stay on the air; they do not preach the Cross.[23]

The indictment about promotion and marketing has five major charges.[24] Marketing meets human needs, and the electronic pulpiteers know how to use marketing to do that. First, they utilize "market segmentation." They have studied their audience, they know it is fundamentalist/evangelical, politically conservative. Some viewers prefer a healing emphasis, some want patriotic expressions, others respond to moralist preachings, and others see themselves as victims of a voracious government or overseas imperialists. The television preachers focus on these varied segments of the markets; those who watch are those who "are already predisposed to accept the message."

Second is product development. The electronic preachers, like secular promoters, promise the benefits which will accrue from accepting the product. The products over the air waves are eternal life, health and wealth, victory over secular humanism, a return to the morality of an earlier age. In short, they provide a variety of products which appeal to the several needs and interests of the audience.

66

Third is pricing. Experience has convinced the leading ministers that their best support comes from their longest supporters. They thus create a "brand loyalty" to their program. The longer the viewer watches, the more he contributes, the more apt he will be to stay loyal to his brand, the spokesman.

Fourth is distribution. Here the electronic preachers enjoy a marked competitive advantage over the local ministers. The latter cannot or will not duplicate the promises or rewards which are made from the electronic pulpits. By direct delivery the latter can offer instant benefits via television or the telephone. These seem personal; viewers are likely to believe the product being distributed is being beamed directly at each of them. To confirm that belief, they can call the 800 number and someone will talk with them. That is simply not possible in the local parish. Distribution by electronics is instant, direct, and persuasive.

Finally, the critics say, the electronic churches duplicate secular marketing in advertising and sales promotion. As inducements to win viewers, the best known pulpiteers offer premiums—booklets, study Bibles, pins, the American flag, or religious lapel buttons. The requester's name and address goes on the computerized mailing list, and the promotion for other products and contributions is under way. These premiums are not for sale—that might sound too commercial. Rather the premiums are available for a free-will offering or are simply free. According to this critic, these religious broadcasters "have apparently copied the practice of commercial marketers in selling the consumer benefits rather than the product themselves." Even when the viewers learn of criticisms such as those raised in this chapter, they pay little attention; they have experienced consumer satisfaction.[25]

In summary, the electronic church has taken a solid hold in American religious life; its growth potential at this point is not yet reached. Its leaders in 1980 could well have continued to offer the original programs by which they first reached national recognition. But in that year, as we will now explore, they chose in varying degrees of explicitness, to involve their activities in national politics, candidates, and issues. The politics of moralism now had millions of viewers sending in fresh contributions. It needed one more ingredient, professional organizing skills. That, too, would be provided.

_____Nine_____

Expanding the Base:
Direct Mailers and
the Politics of Moralism

The New Christian Right entered into American life during the late 1970s because it effectively drew on a wide variety of sources of support, provided a concrete agenda for members' actions, and offered them hope for genuine public power in the near future. The ingredients for such a movement had been available for some years; these included loyal supporters, adequate cash, up-to-date communications technology, the common enemies of liberalism and secular humanism, and a potential audience of millions of followers united behind the television preachers.

Such potential strength already had attracted the interest of a small but well-organized and endowed group of professional fund raisers and vote solicitors in Washington, D.C. They and the electronic church leaders found each other during these years. The mutual interests and mutual attraction proved irresistible; the first offspring would be the New Christian Right.

Like any new life, the movement needed two parents. Joining the electronic church as the partner were the direct mailers, the experts specializing in producing money and political support for specific candidates, causes, and political parties. United by common loyalty to right-wing ideology, the direct mailers made skillful use of computerized, cross-referenced mailing lists and grassroots workshops teaching amateurs how to get out the vote and the funds. Their services would prove to be as invaluable as those of the preachers to the appearance of the New Christian Right.

THE 1976 ELECTION

The first plans for mobilizing the audiences of the television preachers for politically conservative candidates appeared on the drawing boards of Richard Vigurie and Paul Weyrich in 1976. During the campaign they made a few trial runs at direct-mail support for specific candidates, but met with inconclusive results. The analysis by their staffs of the Jimmy Carter victory over President Ford convinced them this bloc was showing clear signs of breaking out from its earlier cultural isolation. Now something like "the evangelical voter bloc" seemed a reality and a potential source for solicitation. For confirmation the mailers needed only to look at the conclusions of James L. Sullivan, national president of the Southern Baptist Convention, the nation's largest conservative religious denomination. He commented, "There never was a time when our nation sensed the need for what Baptists can deliver more than now. If we do not seize this opportunity, I think God's condemnation will be upon us." [1]

PREPARING FOR 1980

After the 1976 election, the National Conservative Political Action Committee, the umbrella organization for a host of special, one-issue direct-mail campaign groups, started up its machinery for the 1980 campaigns. It carefully watched the national opinion polls indicating potential voter interest. The Gallup Polls in 1977, for instance, showed Americans becoming increasingly worried over threats to family stability—threats such as alcohol, drugs, television, violence, pornography, and homosexuality. Those fears, plus rapidly growing anger over the number of abortions performed in the country, increased rapidly in the next two years.[2] The mailers noticed also that evangelicals/fundamentalists perceived that the Democratic Party during the 1972 campaign had "embarked on an ideological journey to the left." They believed the Democrats had accepted the presence of homosexuals, that Democrats believed American values were not superior to those of other nations, that Democrats were responsible for abortions now numbering over one million annually, that Democrats endorsed the Equal Rights Amendment—in summary, the Democrats were "a leftist coalition."[3] Underlying the backlash of resentment, the mailers noticed, was the conviction of religious conservatives that a different party in power would restore the value systems of the past. To fight back this bloc of voters needed only direction and leadership.[4]

The opportunity for them to do so was well along in planning at the direct-mail offices of the National Conservative Political Action Committee (NCPAC). Its leaders brought together for planning conferences several smaller, largely one-issue lobbies such as the Christian Freedom Foundation and the Conservative Caucus. Specific plans for attracting the antiabortion, anti-ERA, antipornography, antiprohibition of religious exercises in public schools groups were drafted in 1977 and 1978 by Vigurie and Paul Weyrich, director of the Committee for the Survival of a Free Congress.[5]

Then scarcely known outside of their immediate sur-
roundings, these groups, independent from any political
party, lobbied for their causes in Congress and through
the mails. Funds came largely from individuals receiving direct mailings on issues in which the donors had
expressed interest. That support was shown to sympathetic senators and representatives; they in turn employed the direct mailers to raise funds and votes for
their own elections. Two Senators, Jesse Helms and
Strom Thurmond, allowed the mailers to put their
names on the materials sent from the several NCPAC
programs.

The techniques the mailers used were not new, but
the size, cross-references, and funds they now commanded were growing more rapidly than ever before
in campaigning history. Starting in early 1978 the mailers
found they had tapped a potentially rich mine of votes
and funds. Vigurie explained how it worked:

> Moral people didn't get anywhere until they
> discovered direct mail. And now we can go
> directly to our people; people who will be
> with us on abortion or gun control or prayer
> in school—whatever the issue might be—
> through direct mail. We can talk to the peo-
> ple about their particular interests. They're
> not interested in 19 of 20 things that are
> being talked about in the Presidential cam-
> paign this year [1980], that there's one thing
> that really interests them and when you can
> go to them and talk to them about that one
> issue and invite them to a meeting or ask
> them to subscribe to a magazine or come to a
> rally, they're getting involved in the political
> process. I don't think there's any question

that direct mail has reactivated a large number of people.[6]

In 1978 NCPAC and the mailers stepped up their programs to defeat specific politically liberal members of Congress. They selected two targets whom they wanted out and whom they thought they could defeat (they were pragmatic enough not to go after a sure winner). The first two were Senators Dick Clark of Iowa and Thomas McIntyre of New Hampshire. The direct-mail programs also increased their solicitations of the anti-ERA voters, alerted to that cause as the Amendment came before their own state legislatures that year. In all cases—the Senate elections and the ERA lobbying—the direct-mailer cause prevailed. The Senators lost, and ERA was stalemated in some 15 state legislatures. Obviously, the mailers were not the sole source of these defeats; they did, however, realize they were doing something that worked.[7]

ASSEMBLING THE MORAL MAJORITY

Still, the two parents of the New Christian Right had not yet explicitly tied the knot. That occurred in June, 1979, after months of searching for just the right leader and program. Vigurie, Weyrich, Howard Phillips of the Conservative Caucus, Robert Billings (head of the newly created National Christian Action Coalition), and Ed McAteer, a longtime fund raiser for conservative causes, convinced Jerry Falwell to set up the "Moral Majority" action group. That would be the primary agency to mobilize the fundamentalist/evangelical bloc of voters and funds. The prestige of Falwell would give it instant national visibility; its operations would be headed by the experienced Billings; and it would utilize the technology of the NCPAC hardware. Falwell accepted the appointment, stating, "I have a divine mandate to go right into the halls of Congress and fight for laws that will save [a morally bankrupt] America. . . . He [God] has called me to take action." [8] Vigurie wanted its base expanded further, stating it would reach out to "the religious people, the conservative Jewish community, conservative Catholics, parents concerned about the almost collapse of the education system. It's all the various groups that feel they've been beat up by the federal government. They see life deteriorating around them and see the government as the problem." [9]

Moral Majority quickly became the most powerful of the agencies uniting the television preachers and the direct mailers. Its grand design for action suggests how well the planners had done their homework, both in attracting support and in staying within the laws regulating political contributions. The programs had separate agencies, all sharing the same ideology, but legally separate from each other to avoid having their resources audited by the Internal Revenue Service or the Federal Election Committee. The first agency was The Political Action Committee, the financial solicitation supply center with a projected budget of five million dollars to support the specific programs. The second group was Moral Majority, organized to lobby via direct mail in Congress. Third, came the "Moral Majority Foundation" to coordinate voter registration. Finally, the Moral Majority Legal Defense Fund was established to carry on the operations in the courts when necessary.[10]

By careful adherence to the donations laws, Moral Majority found ways of channeling its increasing funds into each of these groups as the need arose. Most of the energy for Moral Majority was spent in mass mailings, by the distribution of leaflets to church members through cooperating ministers, by Falwell's preaching across the nation on the issues, and by holding workshops for ministers and laity interested in learning how to get out the votes and the dollars.[11]

THE CHRISTIAN VOICE

At about the same time on the West Coast a variation on Moral Majority appeared in an organization calling itself "Christian Voice." It soon made connections with NCPAC and Moral Majority. Led by Richard Zone, Robert Grant, and Gary Jarmin, this organization moved directly and deeply into working for candidates as well as issues. Its branch, "Christian Voice Moral Government," sent out mailings and held rallies for specific candidates; another of its wings came out explicitly as "Christians for Reagan." One of its letters began:

> Do you believe America was destined for the avalanche of pornography, abortion, homosexuality, murder, rape and child abuse that has befallen us?[12]

THE NEW RIGHT COALITION

The appearance of these two nationally-organized groups broke new ground in the involvement of church-related groups in elective politics. Their leaders were saying the things about American life and government policy their supporters wanted to hear. They ignored the taunts of being labelled "fundys" or "extremists" and took the initiative in political campaigning. They succeeded almost instantly because they knew how to get out their message, pay their bills, and keep alive the sense of crusading against an entrenched enemy. They kept before the public their agenda of the politics of moralism.

They recognized, further, the valuable support they could gain by working with the many smaller, one-issue moralism groups around the country, rather than ignoring or trying to overpower them. Both Moral Majority and Christian Voice had overlapping programs with groups such as the American Life Lobby, The Christian Action Council, Citizens for the Right to Bear and Keep Arms, Coalition for the First Amendment (headed by James Robison), the Heritage Foundation, Life Amendment Political Action, National Pro-Life Political Action Committee, Stop ERA, and others. Working largely through Vigurie's "Kingston Group," an informal alliance of most of these and other similar groups, the New Christian Right in 1979 found its way into the world.

NAILING DOWN THE PLATFORM

New and unknown as it was, the coalition could not have lasted long had it not been able to persuade voters that its program would save this nation. Finding political and religious liberalism and secular humanism as the enemies of America, the Rightists offered instead their case:

ANTI	PRO
Family Issues	
Abortion	Censorship of school texts
Equal Rights Amendment	Classroom prayer
Federal interference in public education	Laxalt Family Protection Act
Homosexuality and gay rights	
Pornography	
School busing	

Domestic Issues

Affirmative Action
Big government
Davis-Bacon Bill
D.C. statehood
Full employment
  legislation
Government support of
  corporations in
  trouble (e.g. Chrysler)
Gun control
Indian tribal claims to
  land and water rights
Instant voter
  registration
Labor unions
Minimum wage
National health
  insurance
Open immigration
OSHA (Occupational
  Safety and Health
  Administration)
Situs picketing
Social Security

Death penalty
Deregulation of airlines,
  trucking, etc.
Tax cut
Western land
  development

International Issues

Detente
Panama Canal Treaty
Recognition of Red
  China
Salt II
Trade with Communist
  bloc[13]

Here was a platform with wide appeal, made the stronger to supporters when the leaders added the dimension of "morality" to each issue. Unless a national lawmaker voted on any of these issues as the New Right demanded, that vote was "immoral." Thus the choices for the voters were simplified—yes or no, right or wrong, moral or immoral.

WASHINGTON FOR JESUS

The New Christian Right, now united with television preachers and direct mailers working together, exerted their first mass demonstration of strength during the primary elections in the spring of 1980. Most of these groups, along with independents, came together for a "Washington for Jesus" rally, held April 29 at the Capitol Mall. Stating it was not to be considered "political," its originator, the Rev. John Gimenez of Virginia, wanted the demonstration to rally America to repent and renew its dedication to an earlier code of morality. To add to its appeal, Gimenez named Pat Robertson and Bill Bright, head of the influential Campus Crusade for Christ, to act as co-chairmen.

The crowds turned out in impressive numbers, the count ranging from 200,000 to 500,000. There on Capitol Mall they heard twelve hours of speeches, music, testimonies, and praise. Significantly, Robison and Bakker joined Robertson as featured speakers. Jerry Falwell stayed away, apparently because he believed the original goal of one million in attendance projected by Gimenez would not be reached, and a loss of credibility for the rally's supporters would follow. Also, Falwell wanted more of an action-centered rally and less exhortation.[14]

Despite the disclaimers, the national media interpreted the rally as a political demonstration. Apparently the New Christian Right had not yet been able to convince outsiders of the differences between advocating their platform, which to them was "moral" action, and traditional "political" maneuvering. When the press, radio, and television heard calls on Congress to act on the New Right agenda, they decided this was political and labelled it as such. Yet those who attended were convinced that a significant witness to their faith had been made, and the nation saw their growing strength. Much of the enthusiasm of "Washington for Jesus" derived from the strongly revivalist tone pervading throughout. One reporter noted the many raised hands, the gusty singing of the gospel hymns, and the general enthusiasm —despite so long a rally.[15]

Yet another reporter detected other undercurrents at the rally. Many speakers denounced the alleged military weakness of America and called on the administration to spend more for armaments.[16] Other speakers demanded a return to a "Christian America," apparently something like a religious theocracy. In all the rhetoric the exact meanings of such statements were hard to define. The postmortem of Rev. Gimenez, however, celebrated the expression of convictions by America's "silent majority" at the rally.[17]

Intended by its founders to bring unity, "Washington for Jesus" showed the nation the determination, the fears, and the enthusiasm of the New Christian Right, now fully in public view. The rally may have united its supporters from their various interest groups, but it brought on a storm of criticism by other church leaders. Lutheran theologian William Lazareth stated, "It is ultimately blasphemy to use 'Christian' as an adjective to describe our partisan agenda. There's no such thing as Christian politics. Christ never identified the Kingdom of God with any left or right, male or female, or any man-made creation." The National Council of Churches objected to the rally as an attempt to "Christianize the government." [18]

The strong convictions over "Washington for Jesus" suggested how deeply its supporters and its critics thought about its appearance. The television preachers, well known for their other programs, now brought the full weight of their power into the politics of moralism. Their supporters rejoiced, the critics attacked. Whatever one's personal reaction, no one could deny that the New Christian Right was well on its way out of infancy and headed into early adulthood.

Ten

Targets and Report Cards: The Politics of Moralism in Action

The political campaign of 1980 brought the goals and the strategy of the New Christian Right into full public view for the first time. Little national media attention had been given to the preachers of the politics of moralism until each of the challengers for the Republican presidential nomination started falling to the juggernaut campaign of Ronald Reagan. Starting in New Hampshire and carrying down to California in June, voters gave overwhelming support to the former governor rather than to John Connelly, Robert Dole, George Bush, Howard Baker, or others. In various ways the New Christian Right had made known its preference for Reagan. When the moment of victory, receiving the presidential nomination in July, broke across Joe Louis Hall in Detroit, the last and the most needed green light to encourage the New Right had been turned on. Its leaders were sure they knew their man; he would spread their politics. As it would turn out, they had made an accurate prediction.

TWO NEW WEAPONS

Reagan's nomination ignited public interest in the New Christian Right. Its vast resources, its disciplined organization, its political skillfulness all burst on the front pages and the television screens as evidence of the kind of campaign America would now face. What quickly captured the greatest attention, both favorable and critical, were two political weapons used by the New Christian Right to implement the politics of moralism. Those weapons were the "target list" of national lawmakers to be defeated and the "moral report cards," evaluative standards to measure the morality of all lawmakers' voting records. Neither weapon was new, but neither had ever been widely used in national politics by the Right. Something new in American religious and political life was in operation. The New Christian Right was ready to show America what it had in mind.[1]

THE REPORT CARDS

Following the precedents of several earlier special-interest groups, both Moral Majority and Christian Voice, as well as several smaller New Christian Right bodies, prepared "moral report cards." Just as conservation or civil rights or labor groups had been doing for years, the New Right leaders selected certain pieces of proposed legislation to serve as norms by which to measure the congressman's level of concern for morality. They believed one's commitment to morality could be measured objectively. Those voting against the legislation the Right favored, or for legislation the Right rejected were, simply, immoral. The leaders reasoned: how could a legislator be both moral and immoral at the same time? That was logically impossible, hence now was the time to demonstrate to the voters just how moral each office-seeker really was.

The first such report card came from Christian Voice. It established 14 issues for grading; these included reinstatement of the 1955 defense treaty with Taiwan, restoration of prayer and Bible reading in public schools, abolition of ethnic or sexual quotas as a means of determining educational opportunities (the "Bakke" question), an end to federal funding of abortion, and support for a constitutional amendment requiring a balanced national budget.

A second, less known, but equally representative, report card came from the organization headed by the Rev. Robert Billings of the National Christian Action Coalition. Billings went on to be a high officer in Moral Majority, and during the 1980 campaign moved over to accept an appointment by Reagan to head the appeal to religiously-oriented voters. Thus, Billings' views covered a wide spectrum of New Christian Right opinion. He entitled his criteria "Family Issues Voting Index." Billings' group stood as an antidote to all of the liberalism which it believed had so ill-served the country since the New Deal. This welfare state, Billings wrote, was morally bankrupt. The evidence was found everywhere; "planned parenthood, the pill, no-fault divorce, open marriages, gay rights, palimony, test-tube babies, women's liberation, children's liberation, unisex, day-care centers, child advocates, and abortion on demand. A man is no longer responsible for his family; a woman need not honor and obey her husband. God has been kicked out, and humanism enthroned." [2]

To implement the politics of moralism on "family issues" the Coalition established voting criteria for both the U.S. Senate and House. The Senate "index" included opposition to federal funding for abortion, opposition to school busing, for a school prayer and Bible reading amendment, opposition to sex education in the public schools, opposition to a separate Department of Education, opposition to extending the deadline for states to vote on the ERA, opposition to the nomination of Patricia M. Wald by President Carter for a U.S. judgeship in the District of Columbia, opposition to the Senate's refusal to grant parents tax exemptions for children in parochial schools, for a mandatory balanced national budget, and opposition to federal funds being spent for child welfare and social services.

For the House "index" a few changes were made: prohibition of legal assistance in cases arising out of disputes over gay rights, opposition to a bill establishing a program to curb domestic violence and provide aid to its victims, opposition to the Child Health Assurance Act of 1979, and favoring a bill to balance the budget for fiscal 1980.[3]

Although the New Christian Right was enthusiastic for this political instrument, the indexes elicited immediate sharp opposition from a variety of critics. To some, the report cards were negatively judgmental; to others, the cards omitted issues such as poverty, injustice, hunger, and oppression. To all the critics, the instruments allowed for no explanations by the lawmakers, who now stood rated as being moral or immoral. Critics also noted that four Congressmen who were also clergymen rated very low on the Christian Voice index. Gary Jarmin of CV explained that those four, along with others, received their ratings because they were liberals—the implication being that liberals could not vote correctly on moral issues.[4]

When the report cards received wide distribution, observers noticed they were heavily weighted for conservative causes. The report cards went so far as to rate one of the most respected evangelical Senators, Mark Hatfield of Oregon, very low, although Hatfield had been interviewed sympathetically on the *PTL Show* and the *700 Club;* Robertson once called him "tender towards Jesus." To make their case, two critics showed the wide ideological gulf between the moralism cards and that of one representative interest group, Bread for the World, which had its own report card on lawmakers' voting records.[5]

Senator	Christian Voters Victory Fund	Bread for the World
Armstrong	100	0
Cranston	0	100
Culver	0	100
Glenn	0	86
Hatfield	25	86
Helms	100	0
Humphrey	100	0
McClure	90	0
McGovern	0	100
Nelson	0	86
Riegle	10	100
Thurmond	90	14

Further criticism came from Pat Robertson, who pointed out that some congressmen rated very high by Christian Voice were convicted in the 1980 Abscam scandal. Robertson himself believed the report cards were oversimplified.

To all the critics one of the highest ranking New Right leaders, Paul Weyrich, made a vigorous reply. The report cards were directed mainly to the conservatives in the churches. Weyrich called on ministers and laity to use them, as well as the other political services of the

New Right, to "Christianize America—spreading the gospel in a political context. Even if we should prevail in every possibility from the President down to the lowest state official, our job will just be beginning. We are in this for the long haul. We are in this until the Lord himself comes back and rescues us." [6] That statement distilled into a few words the goals of the politics of moralism.

TARGETING THE LIBERALS

In addition to the report cards, the New Christian Right joined with the other Right organizations to support the "target" programs for specific Congressmen. Christian Voice leader Jarmin explained:

> We have targeted about 35 members of Congress and the Senate who have scored low on our voting record and whom we think we can successfully retire from Congress in November. We're going to do up a little flyer showing exactly how the targeted Congressmen or Senators voted on these issues . . . print up thousands of these and distribute these to Christians as they leave their churches on Sunday mornings. [7]

When asked by Bill Moyers (himself a Southern Baptist clergyman) why the organization was going to do that, since Christian Voice had stated it supported principles, not candidates, Jarmin replied:

> You can't separate principles from personalities in the election booth. You are not voting or pulling one lever for Matthew, Mark, Luke, and John on the one hand, and a lever for secular humanism; you're pulling a lever

for a candidate. You have to make a determination which candidate best represents
your views; we are for principles first, and
when you go into the election booth you
better know where that Congressman and
Senator stands on those principles.[8]

Agreeing with Christian Voice on the target list, Falwell and Moral Majority joined in selecting six liberal
Democratic Senators for defeat—or to be on the "hit"
list, as the jargon of the day soon called it. These were
George McGovern of South Dakota, Frank Church of
Idaho, John Culver of Iowa, Alan Cranston of California, Birch Bayh of Indiana, and Gaylord Nelson of Wisconsin. Falwell commented that the voters "are joining
hands together for the changing, the rejuvenating of a
nation." [9]

Like the report cards, the target-list strategy was well
established among special-interest groups in American
politics. What went beyond established practice in 1980
was the mutual cooperation between the direct-mail
purveyors and television preachers on the one hand, and
Protestant ministers on the other. Estimates were made
that up to 72,000 Protestant clergy utilized parish facilities for voter registration, grass-roots organizational
workshops, and solicitation. The net results of that
alliance can never be measured with pinpoint accuracy.
Colonel Donner of Christian Voice, however, estimated
that these church groups would turn out most of the 20
or so million evangelical/fundamentalist citizens who
rarely voted. Falwell claimed that by September, 1980,
the various groups had registered at least two million
new voters among the born-again and that they would
reach four million by Election Day.[10] By contrast, the

87

Democratic party and the mainline Protestant churches had no comparable machinery for the campaign.

THE ROLE OF THE ELECTRONIC PREACHERS

By the heavy campaigning months of 1980 the two parents, direct mailers and electronic preachers, had created a full-grown offspring, the New Christian Right. However, the means and the extent to which the electronic preachers supported the report cards and targets varied. Falwell and Robison gave full unrestricted support for the devices, as well as to most other New Right campaigning activities. Robertson, in a less direct but unmistakable manner, showed his audiences where he stood. Bakker remained silent on specific issues.

Falwell became something of a household word during the campaign, especially after his picture appeared on the September 15 cover of *Newsweek*. He endorsed specific candidates, such as Rep. Charles E. Grassley (Rep.–Iowa), who was challenging a "target," Senator John Culver. Grassley was himself a lay preacher and had spoken at the April "Washington for Jesus" rally. Falwell called the Republican platform a "dream platform" because of its tough stand against the ERA and federal funding for abortion. He told reporters that he and other Moral Majority members had met with members of the GOP platform committee. One member, however, Rep. Thomas Hagedorn (Rep.–Minn.) said, "I was never contacted by anyone from that bloc." [11]

The Republicans in turn welcomed the participation of the New Christian Right. At least three times during 1980 Falwell or others close to him met with the national chairman of the Republican Party, William Brock. Falwell was in Reagan's hotel suite in Detroit the day of the nomination. Falwell tried to warn Reagan against selecting George Bush for the ticket. Falwell spent much of the campaign season on a national tour under the auspices of Moral Majority, talking up the issues on the report cards.[12]

One incident proved embarrassing for Falwell. In March Falwell told an Alaska group he had talked with President Carter, asking him, "Sir, why do you have known practicing homosexuals on your senior staff here in the White House?" Falwell told the Alaska audience that the president replied, "I am President of the American people, and I believe I should represent everyone." Later, a tape recording of the meeting showed that Falwell had never asked that question.[13]

Robison, with less national exposure, entered into the campaign with characteristic zeal. To his audiences he went on the attack. He called on the moral, the "pro-family," people to get into politics. "I'm sick and tired about hearing about all of the radicals and the perverts and the liberals and the leftists and the Communists coming out of the closets. It's time for God's people to come out of the closets, out of the churches, and change America."[14] Robison's most widely used format for the campaign was the one-night mass rally, usually speaking in cities which already carried his television program. He picked up on the themes of ERA, gay rights, abortion, armaments spending, and the others. After the GOP convention he stated to his listeners that Reagan should not have selected Bush but added, "You don't need to sit here and look at your politicians and expect them to do right when you haven't done right."[15]

Pat Robertson chose a different route. His position on moralism issues was already well known to his followers from his television programs and his newsletter. He stayed clear of Moral Majority, Christian Voice, or any organized direct-mail group. Nor did he in any direct way state he was supporting Reagan. He preferred that Americans fast and pray, "appealing in essence, to a higher power." The one politically-related group to which he belonged, Religious Roundtable, became too explicitly political for him, so he resigned.[16]

Yet his enthusiasm for the president-elect and the New Christian Right themes was unmistakable. Now America could defeat the liberals, the ones who had failed to control dope, pornography, abortion, feminism, and moral decay because they were dedicated to secular humanism. On his program of November 5, 1980, he said liberals were the same as "leftists," "Marxists," and "socialists" and had rejected the principles that had made America great. To stop this he called on America to return to small government, to realize government could not give people everything they want, to support fiscal discipline, and to balance the budget.[17] His priorities matched those spelled out in the Republican platform and in its national convention oratory.

Once the two major forces of the New Christian Right had been joined in their mutual dedication to the politics of moralism, they found a large, usually generous national audience waiting for their leadership. Then, at Detroit, it all came true. Reagan was no longer only the conservative's candidate; now he stood before the convention as head of the Republican party. Victory, for so many years beyond the reach of the mailers and the preachers, now seemed very close. Their candidate would not disappoint them.

Eleven

The Campaign of 1980: Moralism at High Tide

The wave of voters carrying Ronald Reagan into the White House and delivering the Senate to the Republican Party had been collecting its power for over a decade. Starting first as a backlash against the perceived permissiveness of American society and politics in the 1960s, it grew stronger in the next decade, needing only the precise candidate ready to take his stand against the liberals, the humanists, and the moderates. Governor Reagan had made his first bid for that leadership in the 1976 primaries; his availability for 1980 kept the momentum of the wave alive. Hence, his nomination and victory were building long before the television preachers and direct mailers built the New Christian Right. What that movement did contribute to the high tide of 1980, however, was the call for a "Christian America." That had not been present in earlier years; in 1980 it was energizing voters in a way not known since the candidacy of Senator Barry Goldwater.[1]

The Reagan campaign leaders knew Reagan's appeal to the New Christian Right; they recognized that evangelicals and fundamentalists had been motivated to vote as a bloc for the born-again governor of Georgia, Jimmy Carter. The Reagan aides also knew the disenchantment this bloc was expressing with the record of the new president; high on their list of criticisms were inflation, unemployment, a perceived weakness as world peacemaker, and stories about immoral behavior by White House staff members.[2] The Reagan camp, working with the direct-mail soliciters, also knew their candidate had established good credentials with this bloc. In an interview with George Otis, emcee of a Pentecostal talk show in California, Reagan had said, "There has been a wave of humanism and hedonism in the land. . . . I think there is a hunger in this land for a spiritual revival, a return to a belief in moral absolutes—the same morals upon which the nation was founded." For his proof text, Reagan quoted 2 Chronicles 7:14, Falwell's theme text in 1980: "If my people who are called by my name humble themselves, and pray and seek my face, and turn from their wicked ways, then I will hear from heaven, and will forgive their sin and heal their land."

Reagan described his born-again experience to Otis. On abortion, he stated, "I think it comes down to one simple answer; you cannot interrupt a pregnancy without taking a human life. And the only way we can justify taking a life in our Judeo-Christian tradition is in self defense."[3] His position on gay rights, narcotic usage, and pornography all harmonized with the moralism of the New Right.

THE DALLAS ASSEMBLY

Yet early in 1980, as the polls showed, Carter still had strong appeal among the evangelical/fundamentalist bloc. To the NCPAC leaders nothing could be taken for granted. The agenda for moral restoration through political involvement, they realized, must be taken to every church, to every voter. Many of these leaders—James Robison, Jerry Falwell, Pat Robertson, Richard Vigurie, Paul Weyrich, Jesse Helms, Phyllis Schafly, and Philip J. Crane, among others—decided to hold a massive combination rally and workshop for their cause. Using Robison's 56-member letterhead organization, Religious Roundtable, as the sponsor, they invited some 20,000 ministers and laity to Dallas for specific instructions in voter registration, use of media, and fund raising. There the three leading candidates for the presidency had been invited to speak. Carter and Anderson turned down the offer; Reagan accepted.

On the first full day, August 21, some 18,000 delegates had registered. Between political techniques classes they heard most of the sponsors address the issues of the day. The most decisive event for the New Christian Right occurred when Reagan stood before the assembly.[4]

The former governor stated, "If we believe God has blessed America with liberty, then we have not just a right to vote, but a duty to vote. . . . We have a chance to make our laws and government not only a model of mankind—but a testament to the wisdom and mercy of God." He promised to "keep government out of the school and the neighborhood, and above all—the home. . . . By using our own powers, while trusting in a power greater than ours, we can do everything that really needs doing. Over the last two or three decades, the federal government seems to have forgotten both that old-time religion and that old-time Constitution. We have God's promise that if we turn to him and ask his help we shall have it. With his help we can still become that shining city upon a hill."

Then came the magic moment, the words bringing the delegates to their feet in joyous approval. "I know you can't endorse me," Reagan said, "but I want you to know that I endorse you and what you are doing." [5]

The listeners, one sympathetic reporter noted, "were exhuberant in their enchantment." They had in mind "nothing less than the launching of a Protestant crusade aimed at redeeming America, its morals and politics." [6] During that conference Robison, Robertson, and Falwell contributed strong endorsements to the agenda for turning America back to the morality of old. So strong was evangelical/fundamentalist enthusiasm for Reagan that it swept over the fact that he had divorced and remarried, had given less than one percent of his 1979 adjusted gross income to charitable and religious groups, and his children had "set less than a pristine example for the nation's youth." Reagan's endorsement of the New Christian Right swept away those doubts; the time for the crusade was now.[7]

THE PRAYER OF A JEW

As the rest of America heard of the Dallas meeting, they heard not only Reagan's endorsement but a statement from the president of the Southern Baptist Convention, the Rev. Bailey Smith. He told the delegates, "It is interesting at great political rallies how you have a Protestant to pray and a Catholic to pray, and then you have a Jew to pray. With all due respect to these dear people, my friends, God Almighty does not hear the prayer of a Jew." [8]

That comment slowed down the New Christian Right's hopes for a mighty crusade during the campaign months. Leaders from both the Jewish and the Christian communities sharply denounced Bailey's statement, a traditional fundamentalist teaching. The New Christian Right leadership itself perceived that Bailey's comment could be a major setback. Neither could it help Reagan with the general public. Robison, the conference's leader, rephrased Smith's remarks for the critics and the press, "If a Jew trusts in Christ, then of course God hears that prayer." Falwell made his restatement, "God hears the prayers of every redeemed gentile and Jew," meaning, as one reporter stated, "only those redeemed by Jesus Christ could have prayers answered." Falwell replied to reporters that his views were not anti-Semitic.[9]

The other leading television preachers, Robertson and Bakker, looked carefully at the media coverage of Bailey's statement; both decided to stay out of any controversy. Bakker had never been formally allied with Robison's Roundtable; Robertson now formally announced his resignation from it.[10] Reagan himself, sensing that voters were identifying his endorsement of the conference with Bailey, moved to correct the situation. On October 3 he delivered a major address in Falwell's hometown, Lynchburg, Virginia. Reagan carefully limited his remarks to endorsing specific issues (such as restoring religious exercises in public schools) and referred throughout the talk to "Judeo-Christian values." At a press conference in Lynchburg, Reagan was asked if he shared the views of Smith, Robison, and Falwell. He replied, "No, since both the Christian and Judaic religions are based on the same God, the God of Moses. I'm quite sure that these prayers are heard. But then, I guess everyone can make his own interpretation of the Bible, and many individuals have been making different interpretations for a long time."[11]

That did not quiet the controversy. Christian and Jewish leaders continued their criticism of the fundamentalists; Falwell noted a dropoff in contributions to Moral Majority. He then consulted with the American Jewish Committee leadership. On October 10 he made a new statement of his views; "This is a time for Catholics, Protestants, Jews, Mormons, and all Americans to rise above every effort to polarize us in our efforts to return this nation to a commitment to the moral principles on which America was built. America is a pluralistic republic. We cannot survive if we allow it to become anything less. God hears the cry of any sincere person who calls on him." [12] The director of the interreligious affairs of the Committee, Rabbi Marc H. Tannenbaum, replied that Falwell's new statement was "a necessary and timely clarification of his basic attitudes towards Jews." [13]

The rabbi went on to suggest that the incident demonstrated how "wild a religio-political movement can become if it goes uncontested. They're running into a massive reaction they didn't know existed." [14] Pollster Lou Harris reported that the positions of Moral Majority were at odds with those of the majority of Americans. He detected a public backlash against the "overkill" zeal of the Rightists. The New York Times reported a "furor" of protest over the statement that God did not hear the prayer of the Jew.[15]

President Carter picked up the issue, stating that the election of Reagan would increase tensions between Jews and Christians. Through Press Secretary Jody Powell he said Reagan seemed to consider it an issue on which reasonable men could disagree. Carter went on to criticize Moral Majority by name for advocating a "narrow definition of what a Christian is and also what an acceptable politician is, and I don't want to see that happen." [16]

INCREASING THE ATTACK

While Moral Majority slowed down some of its offensive, its counterpart, Christian Voice, increased its attack. Its direct-mail letters claimed that Carter had not truly stood up for what he believed: "Mr. Carter is afraid of offending Gloria Steinem, the National Organization for Women and the Equal Rights Amendment but not afraid of turning his back on his God! This is exactly what has brought America to the crisis point we are in today. *You and I have absolutely no choice.*" Christian Voice called for the election of Reagan.[17]

The New Christian Right needed to defeat not only Carter but also its targeted Senators. The strategy it employed suggests how well it had learned its lessons on campaigning. Calling George McGovern the "juiciest target" for defeat, the New Christian Right focused on a specific number of issues and kept repeating these throughout the campaign. The incumbent was soft on abortion (he was called a "baby-killer"), against a strong military, and "antifamily." Some $300,000 of out-of-state money was sent to the opposition.[18] Another targeted Senator, Gaylord Nelson of Wisconsin, found less pointed New Right criticism of his record. Still another, Birch Bayh of Indiana discovered considerable out-of-state antiabortion funds being sent in; the NCPAC paid for many full-page ads in Indiana newspapers calling for his defeat.[19]

The strongest show of New Christian Right muscle turned up in Iowa. Antiliberal voters had already been organized there during the 1978 campaign by the direct mailers to oust Senator Dick Clark. Now in 1980 that organization and experience gave the challenger, Congressman Charles E. Grassley, the means to take the initiative throughout the campaign. Incumbent Senator Culver found himself on the defensive; Jerry Falwell campaigned personally in the state for Grassley; the NCPAC newspaper ads focused on the moralism issues.[20]

In Idaho voters were still upset over Senator Church's support for the Panama Canal treaty. Church's opponent, Congressman Steve Symns, was not an especially effective campaigner, but his managers focused on the abortion issue; both Christian Voice and Moral Majority spokesmen in the state worked with the Symns group.[21]

Surprisingly, even though Senator Alan Cranston of California was on the target list, the Rightists showed little interest in spending time and money to defeat him. Their campaign lacked the bite, energy, and sophistication shown in the other targeted states. In other states with liberal Democrats up for reelection, such as Oklahoma and North Carolina, Moral Majority and Christian Voice drew on traditional church-related sources of strength to register voters for their candidates.[22]

Obviously, no foolproof research methods exist to determine the precise influence of the New Christian Right in these campaigns. In some cities their saturation in the media was very heavy; in other areas, it was nonexistent. Undoubtedly, in some campaigns the supporters of the New Christian Right would have voted against those targeted regardless of that designation; in others, the targeting hurt the incumbents. And, of course, in still other areas, being a target may well have helped the senator seeking reelection.[23]

BACKLASH AGAINST THE NEW CHRISTIAN RIGHT

Both the Reagan and senatorial campaigns conducted by the New Christian Right created a sharp, escalating backlash of criticism from mainline and some evangelical church leaders. As individuals and in groups they spoke out. A former Southern Baptist president, the Rev.

Jimmy Allen, denounced the "total capitulation of a segment of the evangelical Christian movement to right-wing politics and sword-rattling jingoism." So also did the national Council of Bishops of the United Methodist Church, and leaders of 13 denominations in a united statement, noting the New Christian Right "selection of issues to be theologically and ethically inadequate." [24] The National Council of Churches responded that no one group could claim to have a monopoly on Christian truth in controversial moral issues. The American Jewish Committee criticised the New Christian Right for its negativism and its correlation of theological and political right-wing ideology. It expressed concern over what a New Christian Right victory would mean for religious pluralism in America.[25]

Those criticized, especially Christian Voice and Jerry Falwell, responded. Morality was a matter of right or wrong; behavior was either moral or immoral. The issues on the New Christian Right agenda were not compromisable. It was not a matter of arrogance or special insight; the Bible taught precisely what Christians should believe. For those who understood that, their condemnation of the morality of their opponents was necessary, in fact the duty of the true Christian.[26]

Opposition persisted, however, leading to the creation of two nationally-based groups to counter the New Christian Right. In Milwaukee, Professor Daniel Maguire of Marquette University founded Moral Alternatives in Politics. Members agreed to solicit funds for newspaper and television ads and to send out sample sermons to ministers and statements of their position to legislators. Board members included a wide spectrum of American religious leaders. A second group, People for the American Way, was created by television producer, Norman Lear, the Reverend Theodore Hesburgh of

Notre Dame, the Reverend William Howard, current President of the National Council of Churches, and Rabbi Tannenbaum, among others. The group purchased television spots in 14 cities to voice its criticism of the Right and its plea for maintaining religious pluralism.[27]

VICTORY FOR THE NEW CHRISTIAN RIGHT

The controversy among church people stayed on the front pages up until the November 4 election. Then, in a time of surprises, innovations, and new ingredients in American political life, came the impressive victory of the Reagan-Bush ticket. Winning 51 percent of the popular vote, they carried every section of the country. Equally important for the New Christian Right was the Republican sweep in the Senate; the party moved from 41-59 minority into a 53-47 majority, its first in 26 years. The House of Representatives remained under Democratic control, but lost 32 seats to the GOP.

All the leaders of the New Christian Right rejoiced. Falwell stated, "We feel that we now have a Washington government that will help us do this [banning abortion, curtailing gay rights, resisting ERA, among the other New Christian Right demands]." Jarmin of Christian Voice said, "It's the beginning of a new era of conservatism in America. The outcome means greater emphasis on moral values." Robertson's endorsement was less direct but equally clear. On his post-mortem show, November 5, he explained that the voters understood liberals were "socialists," "leftists," "Marxists," and "believers in big government." The voters said in 1980, "No, we don't want this." He showed on film Reagan speaking to the Dallas Roundtable; the *700 Club* program included those excerpts from the president-elect's speech dealing with faith and morality.

The direct mailers expressed themselves with equal glee. On November 11 on a *700 Club* show Vigurie and Phillips talked with Robertson. They expressed strong approval of the election results and promised to increase the work of their organizations to elect even more approved candidates in 1982.[28]

The authors of the moral report cards expressed equal jubilation over the election returns. They claimed their work had been determinative in the ouster of five of their six prime senatorial candidates—only targeted Senator Alan Cranston survived their offensive. They also claimed they had helped defeat other liberal Democrats not on the target list. These included Elizabeth Holzman in New York, Robert Coats in Oklahoma, Robert Morgan in North Carolina, and Jim Folsom in Alabama. All of those lost to conservatives. However, some states in which the New Christian Right did campaign returned incumbent liberals to Washington: Gary Hart of Colorado, Patrick Leahy of Vermont, Thomas Eagleton of Missouri, and Robert Packwood of Oregon. Christian Voice also claimed some of the glory for the election of 25 of the 30 targeted seats for the House of Representatives.

In tabulation form, the senatorial candidates receiving New Right support came out as follows (this chart prepared by the American Jewish Committee and used by permission): [29]

Key: CSFC-Committee for the Survival of a Free Congress
       RR-Religious Roundtable
       MM-Moral Majority
       CV-Christian Voice
       NCPAC-National Conservative Political Action Committee
       W-Won
       L-Lost

Candidate, Senate	New Right Group	Out-come
John P. East (R.-N.C.)	MM, NCPAC	W
Frank H. Murkowski (R.-Alas.)	MM	W
Earren Rudman (R.-N.H.)	MM	W
Jeremiah Denton (R.-Ala.)	MM, NCPAC	W
Paula Hawkins (R.-Fla.)	MM	W
Chas. E. Grassley (R.-Iowa)	MM, CV, NCPAC, RR, CSFC	W
Don Nickles (R.-OK.)	MM, NCPAC, RR	W
Dan Quayle (R.-Ind.)	MM, CV, NCPAC, RR, CSFC	W
Mack Mattingly (R.-Ga.)	MM, NCPAC	W
James Abdnor (R.-S.D.)	MM, CV, NCPAC, RR, CSFC	W
Steven Symns (R.-Ida.)	MM, CV, NCPAC, RR, CSFC	W
Gene McNary (R.-Mo.)	NCPAC	L
Paul Gann (R.-Cal.)	MM, NCPAC, SCFC	L
Mary Estill Buchanan (R.-Colo.)	NCPAC, CSFC	L
Bob Dole (R.-Kan.)	MM	W
Jake Garn (R.-Utah)	MM	W
Paul Laxalt (R.-Nev.)	MM	W

All the direct mailers announced their plans for 1982 including an expanded target list; now with their confidence at high tide, they were already at work to defeat 20 Senators up for reelection that year.[30]

Some days later, however, other observers gave different reasons for the defeat of the targeted senators, finding few of them were victims of the conservative resurgence. Robert Kaiser wrote that the well-known liberals—Bayh, Church, Culver, and McGovern—were from essentially conservative states; in each case the other senator was a Republican. McGovern and Church were "out of step for years with their conservative western constituencies on many issues." Bayh's three previous races had all been extremely close in a Republican state. The four were closely identified with the woes of the Administration, they were long-time officeholders. The voters wanted a change. Nelson's liability was his age and inattention to political pastures in Wisconsin.[31] A high ranking Republican strategist concluded that the New Christian Right "probably had provided the margin of victory for Republican senators in Oklahoma, Alabama, and perhaps Idaho." [32]

Obviously the most important interpretation of the role of the New Christian Right in politics was that of the president-elect and vice-president-elect. Their respective statements left observers wondering whether elected candidates wanted to continue their endorsement. Reagan said he would seek the support and help of every group supporting him, including Moral Majority. "I'm going to be open to these peoples. In other words, I'm not going to separate myself from the people who elected us and sent us there." George Bush expressed other conclusions. He stated no single group deserved credit for the victory, that no groups such as Moral Majority would have an "undue influence" on the incoming administration. Bush concluded that "a lot of the views of the so-called Moral Majority are not extreme views." [33]

The final decision on how important the New Christian Right had been in the Republican victory was thus left up to individual interpretation. What could be agreed on by friends and critics alike was that New Christian Right had not been repudiated at the polls. Nowhere did their endorsement carry with it the kiss of defeat. Everyone involved could agree that the television preachers and direct mailers had outplanned, outworked, outspent, and outmaneuvered their opposition. Everyone could also agree that in an age of rapid social and technological change, the politics of moralism—traditional, authoritative, controversial—had not lost its appeal for the American voters. In a day when so much in American and global life seemed sour, so much out of control, the

New Christian Right had mobilized citizens long dormant to elective politics and turned them into an articulate, powerful bloc. No one in the country, from the law-makers on Capitol Hill to the smallest donor to the preachers and mailers, could ignore the implications of that. The practitioners of the politics of moralism had made their bid; they could claim they had been victorious. They were ready for new conquests.

Twelve

The Politics of Moralism
in American Life:
Responses and Prospects

The appearance of the New Christian Right is both a symptom and a cause. As a symptom it reflects the far-reaching technological and social change in America in recent years; as a cause it will continue to contribute to far-reaching change in our political and religious life. Television and computers have transformed our lives beyond our understanding; moralism in politics will reformulate our priorities in ways not yet fully clear. In this chapter we will present two things: a balance sheet on what the New Christian Right has accomplished so far, and, suggestions on how everyone concerned with the issues it has raised can find constructive channels into which to direct the new energies it has created. Since the New Christian Right will be active for the foreseeable future, this might be the time for all concerned to explore how the best interests of those involved can be served.

THE BALANCE SHEET

Balance sheets in politics and religion are always hard to come by, as Will Rogers told us in Chapter 1.

The New Christian Right chose to be contentious, out-spoken, and divisive, thus complicating the efforts of those observers who attempted to make a comprehensive, long-range evaluation. Those under siege by the New Christian Right in the 1980 campaign responded with their heated rhetoric; moderation was not abundant.

As the conservative resurgence became clear in that year, some observers standing outside its boundaries found reason to applaud it. The New Christian Right, especially its evangelical and fundamentalist blocs, were cheered for their active participation in the political process, thus recovering their "cultural responsibility" by challenging moderates and liberals for control of the political arena. No more were these people willing to accept passively what lawmakers, judges, and government officials declared was moral and immoral. Now the New Christian Right had taken back the initiative on defining morality, standing firmly on the traditional understanding of scriptural authority for such pronouncements.

Observers hailed the return by the New Christian Right to its most distinctive commitment—its confidence in the inerrant, infallible, verbally inspired Bible. The New Christian Right held that God had created only one morally right course of action for each issue. In 1980 those loyal to that commitment understood that they had a God-given mandate to carry those absolute answers into public life. This was not only their right; it was their duty in order to preserve America from moral decay. Finally, sympathetic observers applauded the New Christian Right for carrying out its programs, such as the report cards and the targets, even when under vigorous attack from outsiders.[1]

These were the items on the plus side of the balance sheet, short in length, but to millions of Americans the only means by which the nation could be rescued. This could not be a traditional "campaign"; to them, like Governor Reagan, it would be a "crusade," carrying America into what Falwell called America's "Decade of Destiny."

The enthusiasm by the New Christian Right generated equally spirited and critical reactions by those opposed to its programs. Their list of minuses on the balance sheet came from a wide variety of sources but was never shaped into a single, unified set of objections. Yet by the end of the campaign the critics' case was clear; it is presented here in no necessary ranking of importance.

A major New Christian Right demand has been to get the government out of people's lives. Richard Vigurie claimed the new conservative coalition consisted of people who were beat up and fed up by the government's running their lives. Yet observers noticed that the New Christian Right people "do not want government intervention when their own freedoms are at stake, but they are willing to use the power of the government to force life-style changes on others." These observers continue: a citizen need not be for abortion or gay rights to see the inconsistency. They state, "If it is not right to use the government to force one group to tolerate the life-style of others, then it is equally wrong to use the government to compel the second group to tolerate the life-style of the first." [2] The conservative columnist William Safire noticed this dilemma; the Rightists wanted to remove the government from the private sector, yet have it govern such intimate matters as abortion, sexual life-styles, and prayer. This could well lead, he stated, to a punitive state, one prepared to punish those expressing sexual differences or punish an unmarried pregnant girl. Such would be awesome powers for a government over the lives of the individual.[3]

Virtually every critic perceived the New Christian Right to be presenting oversimplified, emotionally loaded solutions to complex problems. Often symptoms, rather than causes, were the center of the New Christian Right concerns: the rights of the unborn baby but not of the mother, or the belief that since one interpretation of the book of Revelation indicates that war with the Soviets is inevitable, the United States must prepare for war rather than continue negotiations.[4] The New Christian Right, critics say, sees the world as divided into two exclusive camps—the chosen of God and the atheistic communists. Such a dichotomy makes peaceful coexistence virtually impossible.[5] *Christianity Today* editors commented that America is a very complex society and "rarely are neat, pat answers the best solutions" to the intricate problems, especially when they are "shrill emotional cries" (e.g., Senator McGovern being called a "baby killer"). Such attitudes, the critics argue, lead to a posture of self-righteousness and a failure by the spokesmen to be to any degree self-critical.[6]

Among the most searching objections is that the New Christian Right proposes its program as the *only* Christian position on the issue, while in reality it advocates a highly ideological political conservatism.[7] It claims full and exclusive biblical sanction for all its demands, insisting that those who disagree are immoral and hence not within the ranks of the Christian family. To the outsider, the New Christian Right does not accept the fact that they have "baptized a particular ideological perspective" with the name "Christian." They have the fundamentalists' assurance that they have an exclusive insight into every biblical teaching on morality, both private and public. In fact, critics claim, the will of God has been reinterpreted over the centuries, refined by using improved textual insights, and always beyond the full grasp of any seeker, no matter how devout.[8]

Observers also worry that the New Christian Right is calling for the American nation-state to become an instrument for doing God's will on earth, a possibility which would threaten the freedom-of-religion clause. Throughout all parts of the New Christian Right is a heavy infusion of civil religion, a linking of America's secular interests with those of the Creator. This linkage lacks "an understanding of the reality of the church as distinct from every nation and as loyal to the kingdom of God which judges all earthly kingdoms." [9] Using fundamentalist interpretations of passages such as 2 Chron. 7:14, the New Christian Right admits to no difference between God's work with the theocratic Old Testament Israel and his work with the United States. In New Christian Right iconography the flag and the cross are easily interchangeable. Critics insist God has no special obligation to bestow special dispensations or blessings on America or any other nation; all seekers are equal in his eyes. A Southern Baptist spokesman, Bill Elder of its Christian Life Commission, states, "There are a good many people who see government as a good way to make this nation Christian, particularly the kind of Christianity they buy. And that's more than infringing on separation of church and state, that's using the state to propagate one's faith." [10]

Finally critics object to the report cards and goals of the New Christian Right being extremely limited in portraying what a truly moral person would support. The lists omit such grave problems as hunger, poverty, unemployment, injustice, oppression, racism, sexism, and protection of the environment. These are the causes of the problems which the New Christian Right attacks. Its agenda to observers seems far removed from the agenda of the Beatitudes, focusing as they do on humility, meekness, and peacemaking.[11]

PRESERVING RELIGIOUS FREEDOM

The balance of this chapter addresses itself to those questions raised in Chapter 1. It offers suggestions on what Americans of all persuasions might do to move us towards a fresh understanding of how to preserve the blessings of religious freedom.

First, as bitter and divisive as the 1980 campaign was, it could serve everyone concerned with a model of what can go wrong when polarization rather than consensus becomes the goal. This was graphically illustrated by the furor over the remark that God did not hear the prayer of the Jew, or Falwell's invention of a conversation with President Carter, or the labelling of Falwell as an "American Ayatollah" by a member of the president's cabinet. Spirited, vigorous exchange of viewpoints is always welcome. Labels, stereotypes, and rhetorical venom will only produce more of the same.

That conclusion sounds reasonable, but given the extent of emotional involvement by the moralism question, can it be even partially achieved? The answer at this moment must be mostly negative. As in the 1850s when Americans would not and could not agree over the issue of chattel slavery and hence refused to work within the framework of existing political institutions, so in our day Americans are showing ominous signs of not being willing to accept traditional means of changing public policy. Religious freedom is the foundational issue, and both sides claim their religious freedom is being destroyed by their opposition's demands on abortion, women's rights, religious exercises in the public schools, and the other

110

issues. What is believed as God's will by one is seen as self-serving ideology by the other.

Traditional means for changing public policy have included electing candidates pledged to specific reforms, carrying one's grievances through the judicial processes to the Supreme Court, proposing amendments to the Constitution, and mobilizing public opinion on one or a set of issues to "send a message" to lawmakers and judges. Today the politics of moralism and its resulting backlash have convinced voters that these means are no longer adequate. Courts and legislatures seem remote, insensitive agencies under pressure to "politics," but not to the authoritative Word of God or to the dictates of the liberal conscience. Hence, stalemate continues over how Americans should go about changing public policy; ill will continues to increase.

Again a question must be asked: do we want to make far-reaching changes in the manner in which we resolve major issues? At this point, the answer must again be negative. The structures and means by which social conflict is resolved are not in danger of being overthrown. What is causing the stalemate and ill will is the fragmentation, what Kevin Phillips calls the "Balkanization," of American life into single-issue crusades. So committed are we to one or two issues that we fail to keep the common good of all of the populace at the forefront. When we in our particular bloc fail or are thwarted, we either redouble our efforts with heated rhetoric, or we decide nothing can be done and give the field to the opponents. The 52.3 percent of total voter turnout in the 1980 election sends out a powerful message of indifference.

But despair is always the worst enemy. No matter what the immediate pressures are for far-reaching transformations of public and private morality based on the norms of one vigorous interest group, America's future will best be served by maintaining rigorous protection of its religious pluralism and freedom of choice.

THE ROLE OF THE LOCAL CONGREGATION

In this respect I propose here something not new but whose potential for directing morality in politics into constructive channels has been only partially utilized. This centers around expanding the mission of the local congregation or synagogue to greater public leadership and public involvement in community issues. The following proposal will not be well received by those who find the central—and to some, the only—purpose of the churches to be a focal point for worship, theological education, and social fellowship. Obviously those dimensions of organized religious life must never be sacrificed. But today the degree to which moral, social, and economic issues have come to dominate the agenda of Americans, including those in the organized communities of faith, requires new commitments for the churches, starting at the local level.

What is being proposed here is that churches reclaim their traditional role, not as *enforcers* but as *examples* of committed faith, in a day of moral relativism, oppression, and exploitation of human and natural resources. That this will not be easy is explainable by the Will Rogers quotation in Chapter 1; everyone is an expert on blending religion and politics. But the need is imperative and cannot be implemented too soon. The local level must be the focal point because our society has lost faith in the programs of national institutions—government, church, school. Hence, by default, the action starts at home.

112

Perhaps no one would disagree with the proposal in theory, but how does it look when concrete program ingredients are added? Granted that the local church cannot compete with the electronic churches for instant counselling, daily spread of viewpoints, or financial clout, yet the local parish has its own resources and strengths. The parish should not attempt to imitate the television preacher programs or preachers; it has something electronic evangelism could never offer. The local congregation makes available the experience of authentic face-to-face exchange, of immediate personal support for those in need, of proving that problems can be solved and lives changed by one's personal involvement right at that place rather than by identification with a remote electronic signal.

Next, churches can greatly strengthen their educational ministry to emphasize how agonizing, frustrating, but necessary it is to understand God's will for each seeker and for a society which shuns sectarian domination. That means a ministry which is aware of the difficulty of proclaiming with absolute precision what God intends for each person and for society. This task is especially hard in a day such as ours when the staggering complexity of daily living leaves us vulnerable to simple, authoritarian answers offered to relieve the seeker from individual searching. Yet it is an ongoing task that must stay near the top of the agenda. Living the faith has never been easy, predictable, or harmonious with the pleasures of this life. When we realize that we celebrate that "vagrant celibate whose seminar on happiness elevated the mournful meek rather than the smiling success," we will have a clearer mandate for our search, and less dependence on packaged, dogmatic explanations.[12]

Further, the local parish can increase its role in the

113

community as a center for public discussion of the major issues facing the neighborhood, the city, the nation, the world. The new role of the evangelical and fundamentalist ministers in the campaign of 1980 has left the moderate and mainline parishes little choice but to enter into community dialogue. Churches and synagogues can become centers of information for voters on legislative voting records, campaign finances, party platforms—the whole gamut of matters which only one segment of the religious community controlled in 1980. Some readers will say this would be getting the congretions into "politics." I would reply that it is providing a service for the community. By scrupulous attention to balance, accuracy, and fairness of presentation, the churches can have a demonstrable impact on elections.

In another area, the local churches need not inevitably surrender money, loyalty, and dedication from its members to the national electronic churches who are meeting personal needs. Again, the local parish has resources and means for nurture which television cannot begin to duplicate. For instance, some parishes have introduced "cluster" communities within their membership. These include voluntary commitments by singles or families of from five to twenty people to show special, direct, usually daily involvement in a variety of ways with one another —prayer, sharing, listening, loaning—the list is as long as the imagination of the participants. In this complex society the cluster group admits its dependency on other people and finds strength in depending on those they can see, hear, and know in their immediate community. In a related field, the great success of the retreat ministry in programs such as Marriage Encounter suggests the ongoing popularity of small-group retreats for a day, a weekend, or other time period for support and nurture among trusting friends.

114

For denominations willing to make the effort, those persons who have opted for watching Sunday services on home television (and the shut-ins, of course) could be given the alternative to national celebrities by viewing regionally broadcast worship services. The focus would be on the congregation's activities, not on a famous preacher or "show-biz" effects. The national denominations could also make available to a far greater degree than at present educational and worship programs on video cassettes and similar technology for use at home or in the local parish. Some groups have started this; the potential for using such technology to strengthen one's denominational and local parish commitment are virtually boundless.[13]

Beyond these suggestions, churches and synagogues have the opportunity to provide the laity and clergy with an understanding of what is wrong and what is right about commercial and public television. Manipulated by skillful advertising and image making, people are vulnerable to the message of success and power which the advertisers promote on the screen. The churches could do more to show that "God is on the side of the poor and powerless," that friendship does not depend upon deodorants, nor contentment on automobile ownership. The best place for such education, one specialist argues, is in the church, "one of the few places in society where people regularly come together on a face-to-face basis."[14]

THE UNRESOLVED AGENDA

In summary, the appearance of the New Christian Right, advocating its politics of moralism, reflects long-standing grievances and the utilization of communications technology which have challenged traditional political and moral institutions throughout the nation. Questions long dormant, such as what is right and wrong, who decides, how are dissenting rights protected, what are acceptable ethics in promotion, fund raising, and proselytization have fueled long-smoldering fires of resentment and bitterness throughout American life. Patterns of behavior, such as evangelical avoidance of political involvement, or complex issues long avoided in public discourse, such as homosexuality, were rejected in 1980 in favor of the new involvement. Moral issues of excruciating complexity were injected into political campaigning, thus suggesting a majority vote on an issue was the final authority on whether that issue was moral or immoral. Thus, times were not one of unity, one for celebrating oneness in Christ, the strength from all being of the same body.

The political results were compelling enough to convince the New Christian Right that its power was being felt, its voice determinative, its future bright for achieving full control to create a Christian America. Yet with its speed in growth, its strength of resources, its assurance in knowing what was and what was not moral, the New Christian Right movement engendered opposition from both the secular and church-related worlds. Will Rogers was right: Americans do not like to be told the precise blend of religion and politics.

So long as the issues on the agenda remain unsolved, so long as citizens are willing to contribute and organize and vote, so long as the world continues to seem an increasingly perilous place for its inhabitants, the questions raised by the politics of moralism will persist. And so will the love and nurture of God for all his people.

Notes

1. The Emergence of the New Christian Right

1. I am using "right" and "conservative" interchangeably. We can readily find many shadings of differences between the two terms, but as a working definition, they will do well.
2. See, among the many definitions, Austin Fagothey, *Right and Reason: Ethics in Theory and Practice* (St. Louis: The C. V. Mosby Company, 1976), p. 47.

2. The Christian Right: Transformation from Old to New

1. See Elwyn Smith, *Religious Liberty in the United States* (Philadelphia: Fortress Press, 1972), Chap. 14; Anson Phelps Stokes and Leo Pfeffer, *Church and State in the United States* (N.Y.: Harper & Row, 1964), Chaps. 4-5. Among the better known persecuted groups have been the Anabaptists, Mormons, and Roman Catholics.
2. For a complete list, see Chap. 9.
3. For one account, see Erling Jorstad, *The Politics of Doomsday: Fundamentalists of the Far Right* (Nashville: Abingdon Press, 1970).
4. *Ibid.*, esp. Chaps. 6-7.
5. From the television program, *Bill Moyers' Journal*, Sept. 28, 1980.
6. The speech is in *Christianity Today*, July 31, 1970, pp. 988-89; Lowell Streiker and Gerald Strober, *Religion and the New Majority* (N.Y.: Association Press, 1972), pp. 70-77.
7. Dean Kelley, *Why Conservative Churches Are Growing* (N.Y.: Harper & Row, 1972, rev. ed., 1978); news story, *New York Times*, March 9, 1975, pp. 1, 35; George Gallup and David

Poling, *The Search for America's Faith* (Nashville: Abingdon Press, 1980), pp. 133-39; C. Peter Wagner, "How 'Christian' Is America?," *Christianity Today*, Dec. 3, 1976, p. 280.

8. "Bringing the Word," *New York Times Sunday Book Review,* March 3, 1978, p. 5; *Publisher's Weekly*, March 14, 1977, pp. 82-83; see my Chap. 10, "Revival Across the Land," in *Evangelicals in the White House: The Cultural Maturation of Evangelism in America, 1960-1981.*(N.Y.: Edwin Mellen Press, 1981).

9. Albert J. Menendez, *Religion at the Polls* (Philadelphia: The Westminster Press, 1977); pp. 181-205; Jorstad, *Evangelicals,* Chap. 7.

10. See the documentation in David O. Moberg, *The Great Reversal: Evangelism Versus Social Concern* (Philadelphia: J. B. Lippincott Co., 1972).

11. Jim Wallis and Wes Michaelsen, "Building Up the Common Life," *Sojourners*, April, 1976, vol. 4, p. 4.

12. *Ibid.*

13. *Ibid.*, p. 11.

14. *Ibid.*, p. 12.

15. Phillips, "The Balkanization of America," *Harper's*, May, 1978, pp. 37-47; Moyers' interview with Vigurie and Weyrich on *Bill Moyers' Journal*, Sept. 28, 1980.

3. Evangelism by Electronics: The Rise of the Television Churches

1. Lawrence P. Wynne, "The Next Stage in Satellite Communications," *Religious Broadcasting*, June/July, 1978, p. 17.

2. Robert M. Liebert, "The Electronic Church: A Psychological Perspective," pp. 1, 23. This is a paper (also available on cassette tape) given at the "Electronic Church Consultation," New York University, Feb. 6-7, 1980, sponsored by the Communications Commission, National Council of Churches (all papers are available from Room 860, N.C.C.); hereafter papers from this conference are referred to as "Electronic Church Consultation."

3. Ben Armstrong, *The Electric Church* (Nashville: Thomas Nelson Publishers, 1979), pp. 19-20.

4. *Ibid.*, pp. 21-25.

5. *Ibid.*, p. 19.

6. *Ibid.*, p. 24, and Chaps. 2-5.

7. *Ibid.*, Chaps. 6-8; Virginia Stem Owens, *The Total Image: Or Selling Jesus in the Modern Age* (Grand Rapids: Wm. B. Eerdmans Co., 1980), Chap. 2.

8. Jeffrey K. Hadden, "Some Sociological Reflections on the Electronic Church," Electronic Church Consultation, p. 11;

Jerry Sholes, *Give Me That Prime Time Religion* (N.Y.: Hawthorn Books, 1979), p. 1.

9. Marshall Frady, *Billy Graham: A Parable of Righteousness* (Boston: Little, Brown Co., 1979), pp. 271-72, 312-14; John C. Pollock, *Billy Graham: The Authorized Biography* (N.Y.: McGraw-Hill, 1966), pp. 237-45.

10. Scott Hessek, "Christians and the Supermedia," *Christian Life,* January, 1977, p. 75.

11. Hadden, "Some Sociological Reflections," p. 14; Princeton Religious Research Center, *Emerging Trends,* Oct., 1980, vol. 2, no. 8, p. 3; George Gallup Jr. and David Poling, *The Search for America's Faith* (Nashville: Abingdon Press, 1980), pp. 116-124; "Born Again," *Newsweek,* Oct. 25, 1976, p. 69; Jeremy Rifkin with Ted Howard, *The Emerging Order: God in the Age of Scarcity* (N.Y.: G. P. Putnam's Sons, 1979), pp. 105-14.

12. More critical articles are Michael Barton, "What a Friend They Have in Jesus," *Christian Century,* Sept. 19, 1979, pp. 887-88; news story in *ibid.,* March 1, 1978, pp. 203-04; editorial in *ibid.,* Feb. 27, 1980, pp. 219-20; M. E. Marty, "The Electronic Church," *Missouri in Perspective,* March 27, 1978, p. 5; news story, *Christianity Today,* March 7, 1980, pp. 346-48.

13. Merle Allison Johnson, *How to Be Happy in the Non-Electric Church* (Nashville: Abingdon Press, 1979); Hadden, "Some Sociological Reflections," pp. 8-18.

4. Pat Robertson, the 700 Club, and the Christian Broadcasting Network

1. Information from CBN brochures, "The World of CBN" (1980), p. 3; "Our CBN Center," (1979), pp. 5-6.

2. William Martin, "Heavenly Hosts," *Texas Monthly,* March, 1979, reprinted and distributed by CBN.

3. Dick Dabney, "God's Own Network," *Harper's,* Aug., 1980, p. 47; see a CBN flyer, "A Transcript of an interview with Pat Robertson: How the *700 Club* Began," pp. 2-4.

4. Dabney, pp. 35-36.

5. *Christianity Today,* Sept. 10, 1976, p. 1244; *ibid.,* p. 1260; *Christian Review,* June, 1974, p. 4; *Christian Life,* Jan., 1977, p. 39. By this time Robertson was getting equal promotional billing with such celebrities at the Jesus Festivals like David Wilkerson and several well-known Christian rock bands; William Martin, "Video Evangelism," *Washington Post Magazine,* June 4, 1978, pp. 37, 39, 41; Ed Zuckerman, "Born-Again Broadcasts Come to Boston," *The Real Paper,* May 6, 1978, p. 18.

6. *National Courier,* June 25, 1976, p. 2; CBN, "Master Plan for Life" (1980), an 8-page promotional flyer.
7. The billion-dollar figure is found in Robertson's Statement in the magazine *Your Church,* May/June, 1979, p. 5.
8. *Christianity Today,* Mar. 6, 1978; the statistics are from the newspaper published in Norfolk, Va., *The Ledger-Star,* August 13, 1980, p. 1; Dabney, "God's Own Network," pp. 39-40; see also "News from CBN Fact Sheet," (1980), pp. 1-6.
9. Dabney, pp. 44-45.

5. Jim Bakker and the PTL Club

1. Philip Yancey, "The Ironies and Impact of PTL," *Christianity Today,* Sept. 21, 1979, p. 1251.
2. Jim Bakker, *Move That Mountain* (Plainfield, N.J.: Logos International, 1976), p. 14.
3. Yancey, p. 1250.
4. Bakker, pp. 50-59.
5. *Ibid.,* pp. 106-107.
6. *Broadcasting,* March 6, 1978, p. 3; Robertson, "How the 700 Club Began" (promotional flyer from CBN); Bakker, *Move,* p. v; "Special Correspondence," *Christian Century,* March 1, 1979, pp. 203-04.
7. *National Courier,* July 9, 1976, pp. 16-17.
8. Wayne King, *"Praise the Lord Club* Brings Gospel to Television," *New York Times,* August 30, 1976, p. 25.
9. *Ibid.,* p. 43.
10. Letter from Jim Bakker to Erling Jorstad, June 26, 1978.
11. *Minneapolis Star,* August 2, 1979, p. 1B; Yancey, "The Ironies," p. 1250.
12. Brief accounts are in *Christianity Today,* May 4, 1979, pp. 874-75 and June 6, 1980, p. 712.
13. This information was supplied me by the *PTL* in its *Press Kit* for 1980.
14. Yancey, "Ironies," pp. 1252-53; Bakker, *The Big Three Mountain-Movers* (Plainfield, N.J.: Logos International, 1977); Bakker, *PTL Club Devotional Book* (n.p., New Leaf Press, 1980).

6. Jerry Falwell and The Old-Time Gospel Hour

1. Gerald Strober and Roth Tomczak, *Jerry Falwell: Aflame for God* (Nashville: Thomas Nelson Publishers, 1979), pp. 20-24.
2. *National Courier,* April 30, 1976, p. 8.
3. The story is told in some detail in Strober and Tomczak; in Jerry Falwell and Elmer Towns, *Church Aflame* (Nashville: Impact Books, 1971); Jerry Falwell, *Capturing a Town for Christ* (Old Tappan, N.J.: Fleming H. Revell Co., 1973).

4. Edward M. Berckman, " 'The Old-Time Gospel Hour' and Fundamentalist Paradox," *Christian Century,* March 29, 1978, pp. 333-37; Falwell, *Listen, America!* (Garden City, N.Y.: Doubleday Co., 1980).

5. *New York Times,* August 20, 1980, p. B22; *Minneapolis Star,* Aug. 25, 1980, p. 4A; Berckman, "Old-Time Gospel," p. 335; Falwell, "The Future, The Bible, and You" (Lynchburg: The Old-Time Gospel Hour, 1980), pp. 1-3, 19; Stan Hastey and Warner Ragsdale, "Right Religion: Right Politics?," *Home Missions,* Sept./Oct., 1980, p. 69.

6. Falwell, *Listen, America!,* p. 63; for an excellent analysis of fundamentalists and inerrancy, see Robert K. Johnston, *Evangelicals at an Impasse* (Richmond: John Knox Press, 1978), Chap. 2.

7. See the "Doctrinal Position of Liberty Baptist Seminary," a four-page dittoed sheet sent to me by request; Falwell, "The Future, the Bible, and You," pp. 1-3.

8. Falwell, "The Future, The Bible, and You," pp. 1-3.

9. *Ibid.,* pp. 4-6.

10. From a two-page dittoed statement sent to me from *The Old-Time Gospel Hour,* "Baptism in the Holy Spirit/Charismatic Movement," p. 1.

11. William Petersen and Stephen Board, "Where is Jerry Falwell Going?" *Eternity,* July/August, 1980, pp. 15-19.

7. James Robison and the Evangelistic Association

1. *Minneapolis Star,* Aug. 25, 1980, p. 8A; a two-page "Biographical Sketch" sent to me by the James Robison Evangelistic Association; *Christianity Today,* March 21, 1980, pp. 406-08.

2. *Ibid.; Life's Answers,* October, 1980, pp. 1-2 (Robison's monthly journal).

3. *Christian Century,* March 28, 1979, pp. 336-37.

4. *Bill Moyer's Journal,* Sept. 28, 1980, PBS; Stan Hastey and Warner Ragsdale, "Right Religion: Right Politics?," *Home Missions,* Sept./Oct., 1980.

5. *Minneapolis Star,* Aug. 25, 1980, p. 8A, 12A; Hastey, "Right Religion," p. 71; *Life's Answers,* Oct., 1980, pp. 2-4, 17.

6. *Bill Moyer's Journal,* Sept. 28, 1980; *Star,* Aug. 25, 1980, p. 8A, 12A.

7. *Minneapolis Star,* Aug. 25, 1980, pp. 8A, 12A.

8. Can the Good News Be Televised?: The Controversy over the Electronic Church

1. Grand Rapids: Wm. B. Eerdmans Co., 1980.

2. She quotes Ernest Dicter, an image advertising writer, p. 26.

3. *Ibid.*, p. 37.
4. *Ibid.*, p. 54 and Chap. 4, *passim.*
5. *Ibid.*, p. 57.
6. *Ibid.*, Chap. 5, *passim.*
7. *Ibid.*, p. 81. See also the general criticism, James A. Taylor, "No Miracles from the Media," *Christian Century*, May 30, 1979, pp. 613-15.
8. William F. Fore, "Mass Media's Mythic World: At Odds With Christian Values," *Christian Century*, Jan. 19, 1977, pp. 33, 37.
9. This is the *Electronic Church Consultation*, New York University, February 6-7, 1980; copies of the papers are available from the Communications Commission, National Council of Churches.
10. From the *Consultation* speeches; Fr. Richard P. McBrien "The Electronic Church: A Catholic Theologian's Perspective," pp. 2-5.
11. *Ibid.*, pp. 7-8.
12. *Ibid.*, p. 11.
13. *Ibid.*, pp. 13-14; See also Fore, "Mass Media's World," pp. 36-37.
14. *Ibid.*, pp. 15-16; Cf. the *Consultation* paper, Dr. Robert M. Liebert, "The Electronic Church: A Psychological Perspective."
15. Marty, "The Electronic Church," *Missouri in Perspective*, March 27, 1978, p. 5; cf. George Gallup, Jr., and David Poling, *The Search for America's Faith* (Nashville: Abingdon Press, 1980), p. 124. Marty's reference to "invisible religion" is explained in his essay in Jackson W. Carroll, *et al.*, *Religion in America: 1950 to the Present* (N.Y.: Harper & Row, 1979), p. 83; also see Taylor, "No Miracles," pp. 613-15.
16. *Christianity Today*, March 7, 1980, pp. 346-47; Stephen Board, "The Great Evangelical Power Shift," *Eternity*, June, 1979, p. 20; *Minneapolis Star*, June 30, 1978, p. 2B.
17. Jeffrey K. Hadden, "Some Sociological Reflections on the Electronic Church," *Consultation*, N.C.C., pp. 17-19.
18. J. Harold Ellens, *Models of Religious Broadcasting* (Grand Rapids: Wm. B. Eerdmans, 1978), p. 93; Liebert "The Electronic Church: A Psychological Perspective," *Consultation*, N.C.C., p. 14.
19. Charles Swann, "Varieties and Appeals of the Electronic Church," *Consultation*, N.C.C., pp. 1-3; Michael Barton, "What a Friend They Have in Jesus," *Christian Century*, Sept. 19, 1979, pp. 886-88.
20. Steven Hortegas, "H-E-R-E-'S Christian Show Biz!," *Eternity*,

May, 1978, pp. 32-36; *ibid.*, editorial, p. 5; on the competition, see *Christian Century*, March 1, 1978, p. 203.

21. Franklin B. Krohn, "The 60 Minute Commercial: Marketing Salvation," *The Humanist*, Nov./Dec., 1980, p. 27.

22. D. G. Kehl, "Peddling the Power and the Promises," *Christianity Today*, March 21, 1980, p. 374.

23. *Ibid.*; see also *Christian Century*, Nov. 23, 1977, p. 1103; editorial, *Reformed Journal*, May, 1978, pp. 5-6.

24. Krohn, "The 60 Minute Commercial," pp. 26-31, *passim*.

25. *Ibid.*

9. Expanding the Base: Direct Mailers and the Politics of Moralism

1. Quoted in *Newsweek*, Oct. 25, 1976, p. 70; see the *Wall Street Journal*, Sept. 16, 1980 (vol. LX, no. 232), pp. 1, 19 for information on Vigurie and Weyrich.

2. George Gallup Jr., ed. *Religion in America: The Gallup Opinion Poll Index, 1977-78* (Princeton: Princeton Religious Research Center, 1978), Report No. 145, pp. 6, 100-03; *Ibid., 1979-80*, pp. 44-49, 91, 103; *New York Times*, Aug. 19, 1980, p. D17; Erling Jorstad, *Evangelicals in the White House* (N.Y.: Edwin Mellen Press, 1981), Part III, especially Chap. 11.

3. W. J. Bennett and Terry Eastland, "The 'New Right' Christians," *Wall Street Journal*, Sept. 17, 1980 (vol. LX, no. 233), p. 1; *Newsweek*, Sept. 15, 1980, p. 31.

4. Stan Hastey and Warner Ragsdale, "Right Religion: Right Politics?" *Home Missions*, Sept./Oct., 1980, pp. 68-69; American Jewish Committee, "The New Right" (1980), pp. 1-5.

5. *New York Times*, Aug. 18, 1980, p. 87; *Newsweek*, Sept. 15, 1980, p. 29; *Minneapolis Star*, Aug. 29, 1980, p. 4A; *Wall Street Journal*, Sept. 16, 1980, pp. 1, 19.

6. Interview with Moyers on *Bill Moyers' Journal*, Sept. 28, 1980.

7. *Newsweek*, Sept. 15, 1980, p. 29.

8. *Newsweek*, Sept. 15, 1980, p. 29; *Minneapolis Star*, Nov. 1, 1980, p. 1C.

9. Vigurie on *Bill Moyers' Journal*.

10. *Minneapolis Star*, Aug. 25, 1980, p. 4A; Hastey and Ragsdale, "Right Religion," p. 69.

11. Hastey and Ragsdale, pp. 69-70.

12. *Ibid.; Minneapolis Star*, Aug. 29, 1980, p. 4A and *ibid.*, Nov. 1, 1980, p. 1C; the quotation is from a letter from "Christians for Reagan," no date.

13. Used by permission from the American Jewish Committee, "The New Right," Appendix C, p. 15.

14. News story, *Christianity Today*, May 23, 1980, p. 650; *New York Times*, Aug. 17, 1980, p. 5B.
15. Dick Dabney, "God's Own Network," *Harper's*, Aug., 1980, pp. 50-51. The civil-religion theme was dominant throughout the rally. Participants brought along their "Sackcloth and Ashes Lapel Pin" ($5) or their tinted picture of Jesus healing the crack in the Liberty Bell ($10) offered by the *700 Club;* Dabney, "God's Own Network," pp. 37, 50-52.
16. Phil M. Shenk, "Washington for Jesus," *Sojourners*, June, 1980, pp. 10-11.
17. See the interview with Giminez in his church's publication, *Rock Church Proclaims* (Virginia Beach, Va.), pp. 6-7; Jane Campbell, "Washington for Jesus: A Message for God's People," *Christian Herald*, Nov., 1980, pp. 86-92; PTL, *Action*, July, 1980, pp. 2-3.
18. *Minneapolis Star*, Aug. 28, 1980, p. 4A.

10. **Targets and Report Cards: The Politics of Moralism in Action**

1. The "media" reference is to the *Bill Moyers' Journal*, Sept. 28, 1980; see also Richard Quebedeaux, *The Worldly Evangelicals* (N.Y.: Harper and Row, 1978).
2. National Christian Action Coalition, "Family Issues Voting Index," (Washington, D.C., 1980), pp. 2-3.
3. *Ibid.*, pp. 5-10.
4. Responding to the interview on the *Bill Moyers' Journal*, Sept. 28, 1980.
5. Robert Zwier and Richard Smith, "Christian Politics and the New Right," *Christian Century*, Oct. 8, 1980, p. 954; Ted Moser, "If Jesus Were a Congressman," *Christian Century*, April 16, 1980, p. 444-46.
6. As stated on *Bill Moyers' Journal*, Sept. 28, 1980; Robertson's remarks came on the *700 Club*, Oct. 7, 1980.
7. As stated on the *Bill Moyers' Journal*, Sept. 28, 1980.
8. *Ibid.*
9. *Newsweek*, Sept. 15, 1980, p. 28; *Christianity Today*, March 21, 1980, pp. 406-08.
10. *Newsweek*, Sept. 15, 1980, pp. 31-32.
11. *New York Times*, Aug. 17, 1980, p. 52; *Minneapolis Star*, Aug. 27, 1980, p. 18A.
12. *New York Times*, Aug. 20, 1980, p. B22; see Falwell's campaign manifesto, *Listen, America!* (Garden City: Doubleday, 1980); and an explanation of Moral Majority to the editors of *Eternity*, July/Aug., 1980, pp. 19-20.
13. *New York Times*, Aug. 20, 1980, p. B22; *Bill Moyers' Journal*, Sept. 28, 1980; *Newsweek*, Sept. 15, 1980, p. 32.
14. Found on the *Bill Moyers' Journal*, Sept. 28, 1980; see also

Robison's monthly magazine *Life's Answers*, Oct., 1980, p. 1 with a slightly different wording from that speech carried on the *Journal*.

15. *Ibid.; Minneapolis Star*, Aug. 25, 1980, pp. 8A, 12A; see also his speeches in *Life's Answers*, Sept. and Oct. 1980; Robison's printed message, comparable to Falwell's *Listen, America*, was *Save America to Save the World* (Fort Worth: James Robison Evangelistic Association, 1980).

16. Stated on the Oct. 7, 1980, *700 Club; Newsweek*, Sept. 15, 1980, p. 36; *The Norfolk (Va.) Ledger-Star*, Sept. 30, 1980, p. 1; see also his statement on "Christians in Politics" in his monthly magazine, *Pat Robertson's Perspective*, Sept., 1980, p. 4.

17. Stated on his Oct. 21, 1980, show; Dick Dabney, "God's Own Network," *Harper's*, Aug., 1980, p. 357; see *Christian Century*, Feb. 27, 1980, p. 219, and the Robertson address to the *Consultation on the Electronic Church*, New York University, Feb. 6-7, 1980.

11. The Campaign of 1980: Moralism at High Tide

1. See the column from the *New York Times* reprinted in the *Minneapolis Tribune*, Nov. 8, 1980, p. 7A; James Q. Wilson, "Reagan and the Republican Revival," *Commentary*, Oct., 1980, pp. 25-32; Alan Crawford, *Thunder on the Right: The "New Right" and the Politics of Resentment* (N.Y.: Pantheon Books, 1980).

2. This was Pat Robertson's explanation, *700 Club* show, Nov. 5, 1980.

3. *Christianity Today*, July 2, 1976, pp. 1047-48; see the periodical from the Princeton Religious Research Center, *Emerging Trends*, Sept., 1980, vol. 2, no. 7, pp. 1-2, "Profile of Evangelicals."

4. *Newsweek*, Sept. 15, 1980, p. 31; *New York Times*, Aug. 21, 1980, p. B9; *Minneapolis Star*, Aug. 25, 1980, pp. 1A, 4A.

5. *Christianity Today*, Sept. 19, 1980, p. 1071; *Human Events*, Sept. 11, 1980, p. 12; *Christian Century*, Sept. 24, 1980, p. 872; Robison's monthly, *Life's Answer*, Oct., 1980, pp. 7-8.

6. *Human Events*, Oct. 11, 1980, p. 12.

7. *New York Times*, Aug. 23, 1980, p. 16; *Christianity Today*, Sept. 19, 1980, 1071; Stan Hastey and Warner Ragsdale, Right Religion: Right Politics?," *Home Missions*, Sept./Oct., 1980, pp. 68-71; Falwell's sermon on his Nov. 9, 1980, television program.

8. As heard on *Bill Moyers' Journal*, Sept. 28, 1980; *Newsweek*, Nov. 10, 1980, p. 76 has the statement in print.

9. *New York Times*, Oct. 4, 1980, p. 9; *ibid.*, Oct. 10, 1980, p.

D14; Tom F. Driver, "Hating Jews for Jesus' Sake," *Christianity and Crisis,* Nov. 24, 1980, pp. 325 ff.

10. *Newsweek,* Nov. 10, 1980, p. 76.
11. *New York Times,* Oct. 11, 1980, p. 8.
12. *Ibid; Newsweek,* Nov. 10, 1980, p. 76.
13. *Ibid.*
14. *New York Times,* Oct. 11, 1980, p. 8.
15. *Minneapolis Tribune,* Oct. 21, 1980, p. 3B.
16. *New York Times,* Oct. 10, 1980, p. D14. After the election the Rev. Smith, other evangelicals, and Jewish scholars met to discuss the issues raised. After Smith talked with members of the Anti-Defamation League, one of their spokesmen, Nathan Perlmutter, stated that he was "saisfied that Pastor Smith had no anti-Semitic intent"; *Evangelical Newsletter,* Jan. 9, 1981, p. 1. For information on other Evangelical-Jewish conversations on this matter, see *Christianity Today,* Jan. 23, 1981.
17. A letter by the Rev. Donald N. Sills, vice-chairman, "Christians For Reagan," P.O. Box 7082, Pasadena, Ca., 91101, p. 2.
18. *Aberdeen American News,* Oct. 20, 1980, p. 5.
19. *New York Times,* Oct. 30, 1980, p. B13; *ibid.,* Oct. 18, 1980, p. 7.
20. *New York Times,* Aug. 17, 1980, p. 52; *Minneapolis Star,* Oct. 28, 1980, p. 6A.
21. *Minneapolis Star,* Oct. 28, 1980, p. 6A; *New York Times,* Nov. 6, 1980, p. A29.
22. *New York Times,* Oct. 14, 1980, p. D22; *ibid.,* Sept. 29, 1980, p. D13; *ibid.,* Aug. 8, 1980, pp. 1, 52.
23. *Minneapolis Star,* Oct. 28, 1980, p. 6A; *ibid.,* Oct. 21, 1980, pp. 1, 4.
24. *New York Times,* Oct. 25, 1980, p. 9; *ibid.,* Oct. 21, 1980, p. B6; *Evangelical Newsletter* (Philadelphia), Nov. 14, 1980, p. 3.
25. *Lutheran Standard,* Oct. 28, 1980, p. 26; *Christian Century,* Oct. 29, 1980, p. 1031; *ibid.,* symposium, "What's Wrong With Born-Again Politics?," Oct. 22, 1980, pp. 1002-04; *Minneapolis Star,* Oct. 17, 1980, p. 14A.
26. *Minneapolis Star,* Oct. 21, 1980, pp. 1, 4; interview with Jarmin on *Bill Moyers' Journal,* Sept. 28, 1980; George C. Higgins, "The Pro-Life Movement and the 'New Right,'" *America,* Sept. 30, 1980, p. 107; Rosemary Ruether, "Politics and the Family: Recapturing a Lost Issue," *Christianity and Crisis,* Sept. 29, 1980, pp. 261-66.
27. *Christian Century,* Oct. 29, 1980, p. 1031; *Minneapolis Star,* Oct. 21, 1980, p. 4A; *ibid.,* Nov. 4, 1980, p. 10A; "People for the American Way" continued active after the campaign, setting up fund-raising programs and sponsoring media ads;

see the general letter of Michael MacIntyre, Acting Executive Director, (n.d.), P.O. Box 2000, Marion, Ohio, 43302.

28. *Minneapolis Star*, Nov. 6, 1980, p. 23A; *New York Times*, Nov. 5, 1980, p. A19; *ibid.*, Nov. 6, 1980, p. A29; *Human Events*, Nov. 15, 1980, p. 5.

29. *Ibid.; Minneapolis Tribune*, Nov. 6, 1980, p. 2A; *Minneapolis Star*, Nov. 5, 1980, p. 20A; *Christianity Today*, Dec. 12, 1980, pp. 1510-11; American Jewish Committee, "The New Right," Appendix A; (used by permission).

30. *Minneapolis Star*, Nov. 12, 1980, pp. 1A, 8A, 14A.

31. See Robert G. Kaiser's analysis in the *Minneapolis Star*, Nov. 14, 1980, p. 11A.

32. The spokesman was Edward Mahe, *Minneapolis Tribune*, Nov. 18, 1980, p. 8A; Jim Castelli, "The Religious Vote," *Commonweal*, Nov. 21, 1980, pp. 650-51; editorial, *New Republic*, Nov. 15, 1980, pp. 5-6.

33. *Minneapolis Star*, Nov. 7, 1980, p. 6A; *Minneapolis Tribune*, Nov. 11, 1980, p. 7B; *ibid.*, Nov. 18, 1980, p. 8A; *New York Times*, Nov. 8, 1980, p. 12.

12. The Politics of Moralism: Responses and Prospects

1. See the column by George F. Will in *Newsweek*, Sept. 15, 1980, p. 108; Robert Webber's analysis in *Evangelical Newsletter*, Dec. 12, 1980, p. 4; Robert Zweir and Richard Smith, "Christian Politics and the New Right," *Christian Century*, Oct. 8, 1980, p. 939; *Human Events*, Nov. 1, 1980, pp. 16, 20; *Christianity Today*, Sept. 19, 1980, p. 1032.

2. Zweir and Smith, "Christian Politics," p. 940.

3. Safire, cited in *Christian Century*, Dec. 10, 1980, p. 1211; William F. Fore, "What's Wrong with Born-Again Politics?," *Christian Century*, Oct. 22, 1980, p. 1004; William Rasberry, political columnist for the *Washington Post*, reprinted in the *Minneapolis Star*, Dec. 2, 1980, p. 7A.

4. *Christianity Today*, Sept. 19, 1980, p. 1032; Zweir and Smith, "Christian Politics," p. 940; Fore, *et al.*, "Born-Again Politics," p. 1002, 1004.

5. Fore, *et al.*, "Born-Again Politics," p. 1002-04.

6. *Christianity Today*, Sept. 19, 1980, p. 1032; Charles V. Bergstrom, "When the Self-Righteous Rule, Watch Out!," *Lutheran Standard*, Sept. 16, 1980, pp. 13, 14 (The original title was "When the Righteous Rule, Watch Out!," corrected by editors in a later issue).

7. *Evangelical Newsletter*, Dec. 12, 1980, p. 4; Zweir and Smith, "Christian Politics," pp. 937-40; editorial, *Christian Century*, Aug. 15-22, 1980, pp. 781-82.

8. The Rev. Paul Moore (Episcopal Bishop of New York), a

speech reprinted in the *Minneapolis Tribune,* Nov. 30, 1980, p. 19A; Philip E. Jenke, editor of *American Baptist,* an article reprinted in the *Minneapolis Tribune,* Dec. 5, 1980, p. 7A; Marty, *Context,* Dec. 15, 1980, *passim.*

9. Phil M. Shenk, "Washington for Jesus," *Sojourners,* June, 1980, pp. 10-11.

10. Stan Hastey and Warner Ragsdale, "Right Religion: Right Politics?," *Home Missions,* Sept./Oct., 1980, p. 72; *Evangelical Newsletter,* Dec. 12, 1980, p. 4.

11. Moore, *Minneapolis Tribune,* Nov. 30, 1980, p. 19A; Fore, *et al.,* "What's Wrong with Born-Again Politics?," pp. 1002-04; see the statement by the Evangelicals for Social Action, "Can My Vote Be Biblical?," *Christianity Today,* Sept. 19, 1980, pp. 1035-38; Marty, *Context,* July 15, 1980, *passim;* George C. Higgins, "The Pro-Life Movement and the New Right," *America,* Sept. 13, 1980, pp. 107-10.

12. V. S. Owens, *The Total Image: Or, Selling Jesus in the Modern Age* (Grand Rapids: Wm. B. Eerdmans Co., 1980), p. 37.

13. Suggested by John W. Bachman, retired Director of the American Lutheran Church Office of Communication and Mission Support in *Lutheran Standard,* Nov. 25, 1980, pp. 6-7; see Horace Newcomb, "Communion Through Video," *Christian Century,* Jan. 7-14, 1976, pp. 21-22; Daniel Poling and George Gallup Jr., *The Search for America's Faith* (Nashville: Abingdon Press, 1980), pp. 118-24; Ellwood E. Keiser, "A Humanizing Revolution," *New Catholic World,* April, 1978, pp. 82-87; Kaiser, "Evangelization Through Electronics," *America,* May 6, 1978, pp. 358-61.

14. An official of the Communications Office, National Council of Churches, William F. Fore, "Mass Media's Mythic World: At Odds With Christian Values," *Christian Century,* Jan. 19, 1977, p. 37; Parker Rossman, "The Church and the Coming Electronic Revolutions," *Christian Century,* Dec. 14, 1977, pp. 1167-68.